Evaluating Research in Academic Journals

A Practical Guide to Realistic Evaluation

SECOND EDITION

Fred Pyrczak

California State University, Los Angeles

Pyrczak Publishing

P.O. Box 39731 • Los Angeles, CA 90039

This edition was written in collaboration with Randall R. Bruce.

Project Director: Monica Lopez.

Cover design by Robert Kibler and Larry Nichols.

Editorial assistance provided by Sharon Young, Brenda Koplin, Kenneth Ornburn, and Cheryl Alcorn.

Printed in the United States of America.

ISBN 1-884585-26-4

Contents

Notes:

Introduction to the Second Edition

When students in the social and behavioral sciences take advanced courses in their major field of study, they are often required to read and evaluate original research reports published as articles in academic journals. This book is designed as a guide for students who are first learning how to engage in this process.

Major Assumptions

First, it is assumed that the students using this book have limited knowledge of research methods, even though they may have taken an introductory research methods course or may be using this book concurrently while taking such a course. Because of this assumption, technical terms and jargon such as "true experiment" are defined and explained when they are first used in this book.

Second, it is assumed that students have only a limited grasp of elementary statistics. Thus, the chapter on evaluating statistical reporting in research reports is confined to criteria such students can handle.

Finally, and perhaps most important, it is assumed that students with limited backgrounds in research methods and statistics can produce adequate evaluations of research reports—evaluations that get to the heart of important issues and allow them to draw sound conclusions from published research.

This Book Is *Not* Written for...

This book is not written for journal editors and members of their editorial review boards. Such professionals usually have had firsthand experience in conducting research and have taken advanced courses in research methods and statistics. Published evaluation criteria for use by these professionals are often terse, filled with jargon, and include many elements that cannot be fully comprehended without advanced training and experience. This book is aimed at a completely different audience: students who are just beginning to learn how to evaluate original reports of research.

Applying the Evaluation Questions in This Book

Chapters 2 through 12 are organized around evaluation questions that may be answered with a simple "yes" or "no," where a "yes" indicates that you judge a characteristic to be satisfactory. However, for evaluation questions that deal with complex issues, you may also want to rate each one using a scale from 1 to 5, where 5 is the highest rating. N/A (not applicable) may be used if you believe a characteristic does not apply, and I/I (insufficient information) may be used if you believe the research report does not contain sufficient information for you to make an informed judgment.

Evaluating Quantitative and Qualitative Research

Quantitative and qualitative research stem from different traditions and, thus, differ in purpose as well as methodology. Students who are not familiar with the distinctions between the two approaches are advised to read Appendix A, which presents a very brief overview of the differences, and Appendix B, which provides an overview of important issues in the evaluation of qualitative research. Most research methods textbooks present more detailed accounts of these matters.

While both approaches have long been used in the social and behavioral sciences, the quantitative approach has been dominant throughout the 1900s, with the qualitative approach gaining in popularity near the end of the century. Nevertheless, the overwhelming majority of research reports in academic journals has a quantitative orientation, so the emphasis in this book is on evaluating this type of research. However, almost all the evaluation questions in this book apply to both types of research.

About the Second Edition

Throughout this edition of the book, you will find updated examples that illustrate strengths and weaknesses of the research you will be evaluating. Also, there is expanded treatment on the limitations of significance testing both in Chapter 11 and in a new appendix (Appendix C).

In Chapter 1, Guideline 2 has been added. In subsequent chapters, the Evaluation Questions new to this edition are number 9 in Chapter 2, number 5 in Chapter 3, numbers 3 and 5 in Chapter 4, number 5 in Chapter 5, number 3 in Chapter 8, number 3 in Chapter 10, and number 6 in Chapter 11.

In addition to the new guideline and evaluation questions, you will find increased emphasis throughout this edition on the importance of considering the theoretical underpinnings of studies when evaluating them. Studies that help us develop new theories and contribute to our evaluations of existing theories are important in helping us advance our knowledge of human behavior. While nontheoretical studies (such as estimating the incidence of physical child abuse) are also important and needed, studies that explore theories that help us understand the origins and nature of a phenomenon (such as the origins and nature of child abuse, which would have implications for appropriate treatments for abusers and their victims) are, in the long run, more important than nontheoretical studies. Hence, when evaluating studies, it is important to consider whether they make a contribution to our understanding of theories relevant to issues being researched.

Contacting the Author and Publisher

Your comments on this edition as well as suggestions for future editions can be sent to me at info@Pyrczak.com. You may also write to me at P.O. Box 39731, Los Angeles, CA 90039. Critical feedback will be welcomed.

My best wishes are with you as you master the art and science of evaluating research. With the aid of this book, I hope that you will find the process not only undaunting but also fascinating as you seek to arrive at defensible conclusions regarding what research indicates about topics of interest to you.

Fred Pyrczak
Los Angeles

Notes:

Chapter 1

Background for Evaluating Research Reports

Academic journals in the social and behavioral sciences abound with original reports of research. These are reports in which researchers describe how they identified a research problem, made relevant observations to gather data, and analyzed the data they collected. The reports usually conclude with a discussion of the results and their implications. This chapter provides an overview of some general characteristics of such research. Subsequent chapters present specific questions that should be applied in the evaluation of research reports.

✓ **Guideline 1: Researchers very often examine only narrowly defined problems.**

Comment: While researchers usually are interested in broad problem areas, they very often examine only narrow aspects of the problems due to limited resources and to keep the research manageable by limiting its focus. Furthermore, they often examine them in such a way that the results can be easily reduced to numbers, further limiting their line of vision.[1] Example 1.1.1 briefly describes a study on whether social isolation and loneliness lead individuals to engage in self-defeating behavior. It deals with only the potential for loneliness later in life, uses only college students, and looks at only one type of self-defeating behavior (selecting a high-odds-of-winning or a low-odds-of-winning lottery).

Example 1.1.1[2]
Brief synopsis of a study on the social isolation and loneliness on promoting self-defeating behavior, narrowly defined:

A sample of college undergraduates was given a personality test. Regardless of how they performed on it, a random half was told that they had the type of personality that would lead them to have few social

---

[1] Qualitative researchers (see Appendices A and B) generally take a broader view in defining a problem to be explored in research and are not constrained by the need to reduce the results to numbers and statistics.
[2] Twenge, J. M., Catanese, K. R., & Baumeister, R. F. (2002). Social exclusion causes self-defeating behavior. *Journal of Personality and Social Psychology, 83*, 606–615.

relationships and be lonely later in life (i.e., the "lonely group"). The other random half were told that their personality profiles indicated that they would have fulfilling social relationships, including long and stable marriages later in life (i.e., the "not lonely group"). These statements were *not* based on the results of the personality test, which was a bogus basis for making the bogus predictions to random groups. Both groups were then given a choice of lotteries in which to participate. One of the lotteries clearly had vastly superior chances of a payoff. The hypothesis was that the "not lonely group" would tend to pick this lottery, while the "lonely group" would tend to pick a lottery with much lower odds of winning. Making the latter choice was taken to be indicative of self-defeating behavior.

Example 1.1.2 is another narrowly focused problem within a broad problem area. Note that the researchers deliberately picked an occupation that is stereotypically held by males. However, it is only one of many such occupations, so the results of the research are limited by the fact that only one occupation is used.

Example 1.1.2[3]
Brief synopsis of a study on sexism, narrowly defined:

Researchers gave three different treatments to see if they could manipulate the expression of sexism among college students. Then they provided a scenario in which the manager of a cement manufacturing company is considering hiring a new employee to obtain new contracts by contacting building contractors and foremen in a highly competitive and harsh market. The students were then asked to rate on a seven-point scale whether a man or a woman would be better suited for the job.

Because researchers often conduct their research on narrowly defined problems, an important task in the evaluation of research is to judge whether a researcher has defined the problem too narrowly to make an important contribution to the advancement of knowledge. Making this judgment is complicated by the fact that the narrowly defined research of one researcher might contribute to the larger body of knowledge in which the results of a number of narrowly defined studies are reviewed and synthesized to reach conclusions that could not reliably be reached based on any individual study. This is especially true if a narrowly defined study sheds light on some aspect of a theory that helps to explain the interrelationships among a large number of variables. Studies that have results consistent with a theory, no matter how

---

[3] Monin, B., & Miller, D. T. (2001). Moral credentials and the expression of prejudice. *Journal of Personality and Social Psychology*, *81*, 33–43.

narrowly defined, lend support to the theory. Those with inconsistent results argue against it.[4]

✓ Guideline 2: Researchers often conduct studies in artificial settings.

Comment: Artificial settings are usually laboratory settings on university campuses. To study the effects of alcohol consumption on socialization skills, a group of participants might be asked to drink carefully measured amounts of alcohol in a laboratory while researchers observe their social interactions. To simplify the study so that the results are more interpretable, the researcher might use a group in which all the members are strangers at the onset of the study. Such a study, of course, might have limited generalizability to drinking under out-of-laboratory settings such as nightclubs, at home, at picnics, and other places where those who are consuming alcohol often know each other. Conducting such research in a laboratory, however, allows researchers to simplify and control variables such as the amount of alcohol consumed, what types of people they are interacting with, and so on. Conducting such research in uncontrolled settings such as nightclubs, on the other hand, would lead to results that would be difficult to interpret because there would be many uncontrolled variables (such as the volume of the music or the types and amounts of alcohol consumed) that could interact with the consumption of alcohol in creating the social interaction patterns observed. In short, researchers often trade off trying to study variables in complex, real-life settings for more interpretable research results that can be obtained in a laboratory.

✓ Guideline 3: Researchers use less-than-perfect methods of observation.

Comment: In research, *observation* can take many forms—from paper-and-pencil multiple-choice achievement tests to essay examinations, from administering a paper-and-pencil attitude scale with choices from "strongly agree" to "strongly disagree," to conducting unstructured interviews to identify interviewees' attitudes. Of course, *observation* also includes direct observation of people interacting in either their natural environments or laboratory settings.

It is safe to assume that all methods of observation are flawed to some extent. To see why this is so, consider the matter of observing racial attitudes. Let us suppose a researcher decides to make direct observations of Whites and African Americans interacting (or not interacting) in a college cafeteria. Her

---

[4] The role of theoretical considerations in the evaluation of research is discussed in greater detail later in this book.

observations will necessarily be limited to the types of behaviors typically exhibited in cafeteria settings—a weakness in her method of observation. In addition, she will be limited to observing only certain overt behaviors because it will be difficult for her, for example, to hear most of what is being said without obtruding on the privacy of the students, and she will not be able to question them directly about their attitudes using only observation.

On the other hand, let us suppose that another researcher decides to measure racial attitudes by having students respond anonymously to racial statements by circling "agree" or "disagree" for each one. This researcher has an entirely different set of weaknesses in his observational system. First, there is the question of whether students will reveal their real attitudes on such a scale—even if it is anonymous. After all, most college students are aware that negative racial attitudes are severely frowned on in academic communities. Thus, some students might indicate what they believe to be socially desirable (i.e., socially "correct") rather than reveal their true attitudes. In addition, there is the problem of what specific racial statements to include on the scale. For example, if the statements are too harsh, they might not tap subtle, yet insidious, negative attitudes. Perhaps more important, the statements will be presented in isolation from a real-word context, making it easy for the students to misunderstand them or wonder about their full meaning.

We could continue looking at other ways to observe racial attitudes, each time finding potential problems. We could do the same thing for a host of variables other than racial attitudes. By now, however, this point is probably clear: There is *no perfect way to observe a given variable*. Instead, an evaluator must ask: *To what extent* is the observation method used in a particular study valid and reliable for the specific research purposes posed by the researcher? This matter will be considered in detail in Chapter 8.

✓ Guideline 4: Researchers usually use less-than-perfect samples.

Comment: Arguably, the most common sampling flaw in research reported in academic journals is the use of *samples of convenience* (i.e., samples that are readily accessible to the researchers). Most researchers are professors, and professors often use samples of college students—obviously as a matter of convenience. Another common flaw is that of relying on voluntary responses to mailed surveys, which are often quite low, with some researchers arguing that a response rate of about 60% or more is "acceptable." Other samples are flawed because researchers cannot identify and locate all members of a population (e.g., the homeless). Without being able to do this, it is impossible to draw a sample that a researcher can reasonably defend as being representative of the population.[5] In Chapters 6 and 7, specific criteria for evaluating samples are explored in detail.

✓ Guideline 5: Even a seemingly straightforward analysis of data can produce misleading results.

Comment: Obviously, data-input and computational errors are a possible source of errors in results. Some commercial research firms have the data they collect entered independently by two or more data-entry clerks. A computer program checks to see whether the two sets of entries match perfectly—if not, there are errors, and the data need to be entered again. Oddly, taking such care in checking for mechanical errors in entering data is hardly ever mentioned in research reports published in academic journals.

In addition, there are alternative statistical methods for most problems, and different methods can yield different results.

Finally, even a nonstatistical analysis can be problematic. For instance, if two or more researchers review extensive transcripts of unstructured interviews, they might differ in their verbal summaries and interpretations of the interviewees' responses. Discrepancies such as these suggest that the results may be flawed or, at least, subject to different interpretations.

These and other issues in data analysis are discussed in Chapter 10.

✓ Guideline 6: Original reports of research in journals often contain many details, which are of utmost importance when evaluating a report.

Comment: The old saying "The devil is in the details" certainly applies here. Students who have relied exclusively on secondary sources for information about their major field of study may be surprised at the level of detail in research reports—typically much greater than even implied in secondary sources such as textbooks and classroom lectures. Example 1.6.1 illustrates the level of detail that you can expect to find in many research reports published in academic journals. It describes part of the procedure used in a study of the important issue regarding the validity of mug shot identifications in criminal investigations. Note the level of detail such as (1) establishing eye contact with each participant at least two times, (2) having the perpetrator remain in the room approximately 60 seconds, and (3) presenting the mug shots in three photo albums with two 4- by 6-in. (10.16- by 15.24-cm), color, head-and-

---

[5] Qualitative researchers emphasize selecting a "purposive" sample—one that is likely to yield useful information—rather than a "representative" sample.

shoulder pictures on each page. Such details are useful for helping consumers of research picture in their minds exactly what took place in the study. They are also helpful for other researchers who might want to replicate the study to see if they can confirm the findings.

Example 1.6.1[6]

An excerpt from an article illustrating the level of detail often reported in research reports in academic journals:

A female experimenter met 1 to 3 participants at the door of the laboratory and led them into a small room. After seating the participants, the experimenter told them that she had to leave the room to get some forms. She then removed a set of keys from her purse and placed the purse on a nearby table. As the experimenter was leaving the room, a male confederate (the perpetrator) knocked on the door and asked if he was at the right location for the psychology experiment. After being told that he was, he was asked to enter the room and wait for the experimenter to return. The confederate then entered the room and engaged the participants in conversation (e.g., "Did she say how long she was going to be gone?") until he established eye contact twice with each participant. At that point, he grabbed the experimenter's purse and fled the room. The perpetrator was present in the room for approximately 60 seconds.

Immediately after the perpetrator exited, the experimenter returned and informed the participants that they had witnessed a staged crime. Participants were informed of the nature of the experiment and asked to sign a consent form. Then, participants gave a written description of the perpetrator and made arrangements to return the following day. Participants who had been randomly assigned to the no-mug-shot conditions ($n = 52$) were dismissed after completing the description of the criminal and scheduling a return time for the next day. Those who had been randomly assigned to the mug-shot conditions ($n = 52$) viewed mug shots for the remainder of the 30-min session or until they had seen 600 mug shots. The total number of mug shots viewed was determined by how long the participants had taken to complete the description of the perpetrator and their (self-determined) pace of examining the mug shots. Participants were asked to record the picture numbers of any mug shots that they thought were or may have been of the perpetrator. The mug shots were presented in three photo albums with two 4- by 6-in. (10.16- by 15.24-cm), color, head-and-shoulder pictures on each page. Neither the perpetrator's photograph nor any of the lineup members appeared in the mug-shot albums.

Having detailed information on what was said and done to participants as well as on how they were observed makes it possible to make informed evaluations of research.

✓ **Guideline 7: Even highly detailed reports often lack information on matters that are potentially important for evaluating a research article.**

Comment: When you begin reading journal articles, you may be surprised to find that even major studies on very important issues are covered in rather brief reports. In most journals, research reports of more than about 15 pages are quite

---

[6] Dysart, J. E., Lindsay, R. C. L., Hammond, R., & Dupuis, P. (2001). Mug shot exposure prior to lineup identification: Interference, transference, and commitment effects. *Journal of Applied Psychology, 86,* 1280–1284.

rare. Journal space is limited by economics—journals have limited readership and, thus, a limited paid circulation, and they seldom have advertisers. Given this situation, researchers must judiciously choose the details they will report. Sometimes, they may omit information that readers deem important.

Often, omitted details cause problems when evaluating research. For example, it is common for researchers to describe in general terms the attitude scales they used without reporting the exact wording of the items on the scales. Yet there is considerable research indicating that how items are worded can affect the results obtained by using them.[7] Of course, judgments about the adequacy of the items cannot be made in their absence.

As you apply the evaluation questions throughout this book while evaluating research published in academic journals, you may be surprised at how often you must answer "insufficient information to make a judgment." If this is your response to many of the questions as you apply them to a given report, you may well conclude that the report is too lacking in details to make an important contribution to our knowledge base on the topic of the research.

✓ Guideline 8: Some research reports published in academic journals are methodologically very weak.

Comment: With many hundreds of editors of and contributors to academic journals, it should not surprise you that published research reports vary in quality, with some being very weak in terms of their research methodology.[8]

Undoubtedly, some weak reports simply slip past careless editors. More often, an editor may make a deliberate decision to publish a weak report because the problem it explores is likely to be of current interest to his or her readers. Let us consider one example to illustrate the justification for such decisions: the issue of charter schools, which is currently a topic of great interest in education. Briefly, a charter school is one that is allowed to bypass many of the government dictates on how schools must operate, giving parents, teachers, and principals freedom to collaborate in order to establish processes that may deviate from the norm, presumably in the best interests of the students. Let us suppose that a researcher wants to compare the progress of students enrolled in charter schools with those in schools that do not have charter status.

---

[7] This statement appears in each issue of *The Gallup Poll Monthly*: "In addition to sampling error, readers should bear in mind that question wording…can introduce additional systematic error or 'bias' into the results of opinion polls." Accordingly, this journal reports the exact wording of the questions they use in their polls. Other researchers cannot always do this because the measures they use may be too long to include in the report or may be copyrighted by publishers who do not want the items released to the public.

[8] Many journals are "refereed." This means that the editor has experts act as referees by evaluating each paper submitted for possible publication. These experts make their judgments without knowing the identification of the researcher who submitted the paper, and the editor uses their input in deciding which papers to publish as journal articles.

He or she has this problem: Students are not assigned to schools at random (like drawing names out of a hat). Therefore, the students in the two types of schools may initially differ substantially in terms of a number of characteristics that may affect their educational progress, such as their socioeconomic backgrounds, their parents' involvement in the schools, their motivation to learn, and so on. In other words, differences in students' progress between the two types of schools might be the result of (a) initial differences between the two groups of students or (b) differences in the programs they receive (charter vs. noncharter programs).[9] The editor of an education journal might reasonably conclude that publishing studies with this weakness is better than publishing no studies on this important and increasingly widespread educational reform.

Sometimes studies with very serious methodological problems are labeled as *pilot studies*, either in their titles or introductions to the research reports. A pilot study is a preliminary study that allows a researcher to try out new methods and procedures for conducting research with small samples, which may be refined in subsequent studies. Publication of pilot studies, despite their limited samples and other potential weaknesses, is justified on the basis that they may point other researchers in the direction of promising new leads.

✓ Guideline 9: No research report provides "proof."

Comment: If you have been following closely in this chapter, you will not be surprised by this guideline. Conducting research is fraught with pitfalls, and any one study may have very misleading results. This is not to suggest, however, that research should be abandoned as a method for advancing knowledge. Instead, the solution is, in part, to evaluate individual research reports carefully to identify those that are most likely to provide sound results. The second part of the solution is to look across studies on the same research problem. If different researchers using different research methods with different types of strengths and weaknesses all reach similar conclusions, we can say that we have *considerable confidence* in the conclusions. On the other hand, to the extent that the body of research on a topic yields mixed results, we will lower our degree of confidence. For example, if the studies that we judge individually to be strong all point in the same direction while weaker ones point in a different direction, we might say that we have *some confidence* in the conclusion suggested by the stronger studies.

---

[9] Statistical methods may be used to take account of initial differences between students in the two types of schools, but these methods depend on the ability to identify and validly measure all the important differences that may affect the outcomes of the study. Even if a researcher makes a strong argument that this has been done in a particular study, the outcome is far less satisfactory than would be obtained by assigning students at random to the two types of schools.

A caveat: If a speaker says "research *proves* that blah blah blah," you will know that you are receiving information from a naïve person. Beware. Read the research on the topic for yourself if the matter is important to you. Another statement that is the sign of a naïve or careless speaker is "such and such a study *shows* that blah blah blah." Listeners are likely to infer from such a statement that "shows" means "proves" and that a single study can prove something. Professionals who have studied and carefully considered research methods and statistics will hedge their remarks, using statements such as "such and such a study *suggests* that...," "an important study *provides strong evidence* that...," or "a pilot study provides *preliminary information indicating* that...."

✓ Guideline 10: To become an expert on a topic, you must become an expert at evaluating original reports of research.

Comment: An expert is someone who knows not only broad generalizations about a topic but also the nuances of the research that underlie them; that is, he or she knows the particular strengths and weaknesses of the major studies used to arrive at the generalizations. For example, suppose a school board hires an expert on reading instruction to assist with a decision regarding the emphasis to place on phonics and whole language methods of reading instruction.[10] Members of the board should expect the expert to be familiar with the range of research on this controversy as well as the quality of individual studies on the topic. Such an expert should be able to make recommendations based on generalizations reached by considering the *quality of the evidence* found in research reports. He or she should be able to point out what is likely to be true and untrue based on careful evaluations of the reports.

As you begin taking upper-division courses, your goal should be to become an expert on the topics central to the profession for which you are preparing, and you can do this only by carefully evaluating the research on these topics. At the graduate level, you will not only want to refine your expertise but also make creative contributions by conducting new research. Careful and insightful review and evaluation of existing research will help you become a better researcher because you will learn from the mistakes and triumphs of other researchers. Immersing yourself in and evaluating published research, much of which is highly creative, is likely to spark your own creativity.

---

[10] As you may know, phonics stresses sounding out letters and parts of words. Whole language emphasizes providing a rich language environment (e.g., many complete books, numerous verbal experiences such as reading books to students) that stimulates children to learn to read.

Exercise for Chapter 1

Part A: Review

Directions: The 10 guidelines discussed in this chapter are repeated below. For each one, indicate the extent to which you were already familiar with it before reading this chapter. Use a scale from 1 (not at all familiar) to 5 (very familiar).

Guideline 1: Researchers very often examine only narrowly defined problems.

Familiarity rating: 5   4   3   2   1

Guideline 2: Researchers often conduct studies in artificial settings.

Familiarity rating: 5   4   3   2   1

Guideline 3: Researchers use less-than-perfect methods of observation.

Familiarity rating: 5   4   3   2   1

Guideline 4: Researchers usually use less-than-perfect samples.

Familiarity rating: 5   4   3   2   1

Guideline 5: Even a seemingly straightforward analysis of data can produce misleading results.

Familiarity rating: 5   4   3   2   1

Guideline 6: Original reports of research in journals often contain many details, which are of utmost importance when evaluating a report.

Familiarity rating: 5   4   3   2   1

Guideline 7: Even highly detailed reports often lack information on matters that are potentially important for evaluating a research article.

Familiarity rating: 5   4   3   2   1

Guideline 8: Some research reports published in academic journals are methodologically very weak.

Familiarity rating: 5   4   3   2   1

Guideline 9: No research report provides "proof."

Familiarity rating: 5   4   3   2   1

Guideline 10: To become an expert on a topic, you must become an expert at evaluating original reports of research.

Familiarity rating: 5   4   3   2   1

Part B: Application

Directions: Read a report of research published in an academic journal and respond to the following questions. The report may be one that you select or one that is assigned by your instructor. If you are using this book without any prior training in research methods, do the best you can in answering the questions at this point. As you work through this book, your evaluations will become increasingly sophisticated.

1. How narrowly is the research problem defined? In your opinion, is it too narrow? Is it too broad? Explain.

2. Was the research setting artificial (e.g., a laboratory setting)? If yes, do you think that the gain in the control of extraneous variables offsets the potential loss of information that would be obtained in a study in a more real-life setting? Explain.

3. Are there any obvious flaws or weaknesses in the researcher's methods of observation? Explain. (Note: Observation or measurement is often described under the subheading "Instrumentation.")

4. Are there any obvious sampling flaws? Explain.

5. Was the analysis statistical or nonstatistical? Was the description of the results easy to understand? Explain.

6. Were the descriptions of procedures and methods of observation sufficiently detailed? Were any important details missing? Explain.

7. Overall, was the research obviously very weak? If yes, briefly describe its weaknesses and speculate on why it was published despite them.

8. Does the researcher imply that his or her research *proves* something? Do you believe that it proves something? Explain.

Notes:

Chapter 2

Evaluating Titles

The primary function of titles is to help readers identify journal articles of interest to them. You should make a preliminary evaluation of a title when you first encounter it. After reading the article, reevaluate the title.

Apply the evaluation questions while you evaluate a research article. The questions are stated as "yes–no" questions, where a "yes" indicates that you judge the characteristic being considered as satisfactory. You may also want to rate each characteristic using a scale from 1 to 5, where 5 is the highest rating. N/A (not applicable) and I/I (insufficient information to make a judgment) may also be used when necessary.

___ 1. Is the title sufficiently specific?

Very satisfactory 5 4 3 2 1 Very unsatisfactory *or* N/A I/I

Comment: On any major topic in the social and behavioral sciences, there are likely to be many hundreds of research reports published in academic journals. In order to help potential readers locate those that are most relevant to their needs, researchers should use titles that are sufficiently specific so that each article can be differentiated from the others in terms of its content and focus.

Consider the topic of depression, which has been extensively investigated. The title in Example 2.1.1 is insufficiently specific. Contrast it with the titles in Example 2.1.2, which contain information that differentiates each one from the others.

Example 2.1.1
A title that is insufficiently specific:

An Investigation of Adolescent Depression and Its Implications

Example 2.1.2
Three titles that are more specific than the one in Example 2.1.1:

Gender Differences in the Expression of Depression by Early Adolescent Children of Alcoholics

The Impact of Social Support on the Severity of Postpartum Depression Among First-Time Mothers

The Effectiveness of Cognitive Therapy in the Treatment of Adolescent Students with Severe Depression

___ **2. Does the title indicate the nature of the research without describing the results?**

Very satisfactory 5 4 3 2 1 Very unsatisfactory *or* N/A I/I

Comment: It is usually inappropriate for a title to describe the results of a research project. Use of observational methods, which are inherently flawed as noted in Chapter 1, often raises more questions than answers. In addition, the results can be subject to more than one interpretation. Consider Example 2.2.1, which undoubtedly oversimplifies the results of the study. An accounting of the results should address issues such as: What type of social support (e.g., parental support, peer support, and so on) is effective? How strong does it need to be to lessen the depression? By how much is depression lessened by strong social support? and so on. Because it is usually impossible to state results accurately and unambiguously in a short title, results ordinarily should *not* be stated at all, as illustrated in Example 2.2.2.

Example 2.2.1
A title that inappropriately describes results:

Strong Social Support Lessens Depression in Delinquent Young Adolescents

Example 2.2.2
A title that appropriately does not describe results:

The Relationship Between Social Support and Depression in Delinquent Young Adolescents

___ **3. Has the author avoided using a "yes–no" question as a title?**

Very satisfactory 5 4 3 2 1 Very unsatisfactory *or* N/A I/I

Comment: Because research rarely yields simple, definitive answers, it is seldom appropriate to use a title that poses a simple "yes–no" question. For instance, Example 2.3.1 implies that there is a simple answer to the question it poses. However, a study on this topic undoubtedly explores *the extent to which boys and girls differ in the use of various mathematical strategies*—a much more interesting topic than suggested by the title. Example 2.3.2 is cast as a statement and is more appropriate as the title of a research report for publication in an academic journal.

Example 2.3.1

A title that inappropriately poses a "yes–no" question:

Do First-Grade Boys and Girls Differ in Their Use of Mathematical Problem-Solving Strategies?

Example 2.3.2

A more appropriate title than the one in Example 2.3.1:

Gender Differences in First-Grade Mathematics Problem-Solving Strategies

___ **4. If there is a main title and a subtitle, do both provide important information about the research?**

Very satisfactory 5 4 3 2 1 Very unsatisfactory *or* N/A I/I

Comment: Failure on this evaluation question often results from an author using a "clever" main title that is vague, followed by a subtitle that identifies the specific content of the research report. Example 2.4.1 illustrates this problem. As you can see, the main title is vague and fails to impart specific information. In fact, it could apply to many thousands of studies in hundreds of fields as diverse as psychology and physics in which researchers find that various combinations of variables (the parts) contribute to our understanding of a complex whole.

Example 2.4.1

A two-part title with a vague main title:

The Whole Is Greater Than the Sum of Its Parts: The Relationship Between Playing with Pets and Longevity Among the Elderly

Example 2.4.2 is also deficient because the main title is vague.

Example 2.4.2

A two-part title with a vague main title:

The Other Side of the Story: The Relationship Between Social Class and Mothers' Involvement in Their Children's Schooling

In contrast to the above two examples, Example 2.4.3 has a main title and a subtitle, both of which refer to specific variables examined in a research study. The first part names two major variables ("attachment" and "well-being") while the second part names the two groups that are compared in terms of these variables.

Example 2.4.3

A two-part title in which both parts provide important information:

Attachment to Parents and Emotional Well-Being: A Comparison of African American and White Adolescents

The title in Example 2.4.3 could be rewritten as a single statement without a subtitle, as illustrated in Example 2.4.4.

Example 2.4.4

A rewritten version of Example 2.4.3:

A Comparison of the Emotional Well-Being and Attachment to Parents of African American and White Adolescents

Do you think that Example 2.4.3 or 2.4.4 is a more effective and efficient title? The answer is arguable. Thus, the evaluation question we are considering here is neutral on whether a title should be broken into a main title and subtitle. Rather, it suggests that if it is broken into two parts, both parts should provide important information specific to the research being reported.

___ 5. Are the primary variables referred to in the title?

Very satisfactory 5 4 3 2 1 Very unsatisfactory *or* N/A I/I

Comment: Variables are the characteristics of the participants that varied (i.e., differed) from one participant to another. In Examples 2.4.3 and 2.4.4 above, the variables are (1) attachment to parents, (2) emotional well-being, and (3) race. That is, the participants could *vary* on attachment to parents, with some adolescents having more of it and some having less. Likewise, they could vary on emotional well-being and race.

Note that "adolescents" is *not* a variable because the title clearly suggests that only adolescents were studied. In other words, adolescence is a *common trait* of all the participants—a trait that helps to identify them as the population of interest. (The matter of identifying the population in a title is discussed under the next evaluation question.)

When researchers study many specific variables in a given study, they appropriately may refer to the *types* of variables in their titles rather than naming each one individually. For example, suppose a researcher administered a major achievement test battery that measures spelling ability, reading comprehension, vocabulary knowledge, mathematical problem-solving skills, and so on. Naming all these variables would create a title that is much too long. Instead, the researcher could refer to the collection of variables measured by the test as *academic achievement*, which is done in Example 2.5.1.

Example 2.5.1
A title in which types of variables (achievement variables) are named:

The Relationship Between Parental Involvement in Schooling and Academic Achievement in the Middle Grades

___ **6. Does the title indicate what types of people participated?**

Very satisfactory 5 4 3 2 1 Very unsatisfactory *or* N/A I/I

Comment: Research methods textbooks suggest that researchers should name the population(s) of interest in their research reports. It follows that it is often desirable to include names of populations in the titles. From the title in Example 2.6.1, it would be reasonable to infer that the population of interest consists of graduate students who are taking a statistics class. This would certainly be of interest to someone who is searching through a list of the many hundreds of articles that have been published on cooperative learning. Knowing that the report deals with this population might help a consumer rule it out as an article if he or she is trying to locate research on the use of cooperative learning in teaching beginning mathematics.

Example 2.6.1
A title in which the type of participants is mentioned:

Effects of Cooperative and Individual Learning in a Graduate-Level Statistics Class

Example 2.6.2 also names an important characteristic of the research participants—the fact that they are hearing-impaired children.

Example 2.6.2
A title in which the type of participants is mentioned:

Academic Achievement and Academic Self-Concept in Hearing-Impaired Children

Note that many researchers do not explicitly name a population of interest in their research reports. Instead, they describe the demographics of the sample they used with statements such as "The participants were 100 undergraduates enrolled in a psychology class who participated in the research for course credit. Fifty-five percent were male. A majority (70%) were White, 15% were African American, 4% were Asian American,...." As you read the research report, you may well reach the conclusion that the researcher (often a professor) has no special interest in undergraduates enrolled in an introductory psychology course *per se*; rather, you may decide that the researcher is interested in research questions that may have broad implications for people from many strata in life but used undergraduates as participants in the research simply because they were readily accessible. Likewise, he or she may have no particular interest in racial/ethnic differences but happened to use a racially/ethnically diverse sample merely because it was convenient to do so. In such a case, it might be *inappropriate* to include mention of these characteristics of the participants in the title, especially if subgroups of the sample are not compared with each other in the study. Thus, you will sometimes need to make a judgment call as to whether the characteristics of the participants should be mentioned in the title of a research report.

___ 7. If the title implies causality, does the method of research justify it?

Very satisfactory   5   4   3   2   1   Very unsatisfactory   *or*   N/A   I/I

Comment: Example 2.7.1 implies that causal relationships have been examined because it contains the word *effects*. In fact, this is a keyword frequently used by researchers in their titles to indicate that they have explored causality in their studies. A common method to examine causal relationships is to conduct an *experiment*. As you may know, an experiment is a study in which different groups of participants are given different treatments (such as giving one group computer-assisted instruction while using a more traditional method to teach another group). The researcher compares the outcomes obtained by applying the various treatments.[1] When such a study is conducted, the use of the word "effects" in the title is justified.[2]

Example 2.7.1
A title in which causality is implied by the word "effects":

The Effects of Computer-Assisted Instruction in Mathematics on Students' Achievement and Attitudes

The title in Example 2.7.2 also suggests that the researcher examined a causal relationship because of the inclusion of the word *effects*. Note that in this case, however, the researcher probably did *not* investigate the relationship using

---

[1] Experiments can also be conducted by treating a given person or group differently *at different points in time*. For example, we might praise a child for staying in his or her seat in the classroom on some days and not praise him or her on others while comparing the child's seat-staying behavior under the two conditions.

[2] The evaluation of experiments is considered in Chapter 9. Note that this evaluation question merely asks if there is a basis for suggesting causality in the title (i.e., reference to causality may be justified even if the research methods are subject to criticism as long as the author attempted to use methods appropriate for examining causality). This evaluation question does not ask you to judge the quality of the experiment or ex post facto study.

an experiment because it would be unethical/illegal to manipulate breakfast as an independent variable (i.e., we would not want to assign some students to receive breakfast while denying it to others for the purposes of an experiment).

Example 2.7.2
A title in which causality is implied by the word "effects":

The Effects of Breakfast on Student Achievement in the Primary Grades

When it is not possible to conduct an experiment on a causal issue, researchers often conduct what are called *ex post facto* (i.e., *causal comparative*) studies. In these studies, researchers identify students who are different on some outcome (such as students who are high and low in achievement in the primary grades) but who are the same on demographics and other potentially influential variables (such as parents' highest level of education, parental income, quality of the schools the children attend, and so on). Comparing the two groups' breakfast eating habits might yield some useful information on whether eating breakfast *affects*[3] students' achievement because the two groups are similar on other variables that might account for differences in achievement (e.g., their parents' level of education is similar). If a researcher has conducted such a study, the use of the word *effects* in the title is justified.

Note that simply examining a relationship without controlling for potentially confounding variables does *not* justify a reference to causality in the title. For example, if a researcher merely compared the achievement of children who regularly eat breakfast with those who do not without controlling for other explanatory variables, a causal conclusion (and, hence, a title suggesting it) usually cannot be justified.

Also note that synonyms for *effect* are *influence* and *impact*. They should usually be reserved for use in titles of studies that are either experiments or ex post facto studies.

____ 8. Is the title free of jargon and acronyms that might be unknown to the audience for the research report?

Very satisfactory 5 4 3 2 1 Very unsatisfactory *or* N/A I/I

Comment: Professionals in all fields use jargon and acronyms (shorthands for words, usually spelled in all capital letters) for efficient and accurate communication with their peers. However, their use in titles of research reports is inappropriate unless the researchers are writing exclusively for such peers. Consider Example 2.8.1. If ACOA is likely to be well known to all the readers

---

[3] Note that when referring to an outcome caused by some agent, the word is spelled *effects* (i.e., it is a noun). As a verb meaning "to influence," the word is spelled *affects*.

of the journal in which this title appeared, its use is appropriate; otherwise, it should be spelled out or its meaning paraphrased. As you can see, it is difficult to make this judgment without being familiar with the journal and its audience. Nevertheless, if you are reading an article on a topic on which you have already read extensively and encounter an acronym that you do not understand in the title of an article, its use is probably inappropriate.[4]

Example 2.8.1

A title with an acronym that is not spelled out (may be inappropriate if not well known by the audience of readers):

Job Satisfaction and Motivation to Succeed Among ACOA in Managerial Positions

___ 9. If the study is strongly tied to a theory, is the name of the theory mentioned in the title?

Very satisfactory 5 4 3 2 1 Very unsatisfactory *or* N/A I/I

Comment: Theories help to advance science because they are propositions regarding relationships that have applications in many diverse specific situations. For instance, a particular learning theory might have applications for teaching kindergarten children as well as for training astronauts. A useful theory leads to predictions about human behavior that can be tested through research. Many consumers of research are seeking information on specific theories, and mention of them in titles helps consumers identify relevant studies. If the test of important predictions made on the basis of theory is at the core of the research, the name of the specific theory might be mentioned in the title of the research report. If the theory is important but not at the core of the study, reference to the theory might instead be made in the abstract, which we will consider in the next chapter.[5] Example 2.9.1 shows two titles in which specific theories are mentioned.

Example 2.9.1[6,7]

Two titles that mention specific theories (desirable):

The Theory of Reasoned Action As a Model of Marijuana Use: Tests of

---

[4] As you may know, ACOA stands for Adult Children of Alcoholics.

[5] Qualitative researchers often start with an orientation (such as one gained through personal experience or one based on a particular perspective, such as feminism), gather data, and interpret the data in the hope of identifying or formulating a theory. When this is the case, the evaluation question applies equally to qualitative research.

[6] Morrison, D. M., Golder, S., Keller, T. E., & Gillmore, M. R. (2002). *Psychology of Addictive Behaviors*, *16*, 212.

[7] Flores, L. Y., & O'Brien, K. M. (2002). *Journal of Counseling Psychology*, *49*, 14.

Implicit Assumptions and Applicability to High-Risk Young Women

The Career Development of Mexican American Adolescent Women: A Test of Social Cognitive Career Theory

Note that simply using the term "theory" without mentioning the name of the specific theory is not useful to consumers of research. Example 2.9.2 has this undesirable characteristic.

Example 2.9.2
A title that refers to theory without naming the specific theory (undesirable):

An Examination of Voting Patterns and Social Class in a Rural Southern Community: A Study Based on Theory

___ **10. Overall, is the title effective and appropriate?**

Very satisfactory 5 4 3 2 1 Very unsatisfactory *or* N/A I/I

Comment: Rate this evaluation question after considering your answers to the earlier ones in this chapter and any additional considerations and concerns you may have after reading the entire research article. Be prepared to rewrite the titles of research reports to which you assign low ratings.

Exercise for Chapter 2

Part A

Directions: Evaluate each of the following titles to the extent that it is possible to do so without reading the complete research reports. The references for the titles are given below; all are from journals that are widely available in large academic libraries, making it possible for you to consult the complete articles if they are assigned by your instructor. More definitive application of the evaluation criteria for titles is possible by reading complete articles and then evaluating their titles. Keep in mind that there is some subjectivity in determining whether a title is adequate.

1. The Third Eye[8]

---

[8] Eken, A. N. (2002). *Journal of Adolescent & Adult Literacy, 46,* 220.

2. Catching Up with the Joneses: Heterogeneous Preferences and the Dynamics of Asset Prices [9]

3. The Cover Design [10]

4. Aggressive Adolescents Benefit from Massage Therapy [11]

5. Can Special Interests Buy Congressional Votes? Evidence from Financial Services Legislation [12]

6. Are Differences in Exposure to a Multicomponent School-Based Intervention Associated with Varying Dietary Outcomes in Adolescents? [13]

7. Beating the Odds: Teaching Middle and High School Students to Read and Write Well [14]

8. Students Prefer the Immediate Feedback Assessment Technique [15]

9. Asian American Client Adherence to Asian Cultural Values, Counselor Expression of Cultural Values, Counselor Ethnicity, and Career Counseling Process [16]

10. Lower-Fat Menu Items in Restaurants Satisfy Customers [17]

11. Designing Emotionally Sound Instruction: An Empirical Validation of the FEASP Approach [18]

12. An Analysis of School Board Members [19]

13. Police Lineups: Data, Theory, and Policy [20]

---

[9] Chan, Y. L., & Kogan, L. (2002). *Journal of Political Economy, 110,* 1255.

[10] Hamby, S. M. S. (2002). *The Library Quarterly, 2,* 205.

[11] Diego, M. A. et al. (2002). *Adolescence, 37,* 597.

[12] Stratmann, T. (2002). *The Journal of Law & Economics, XLV,* 345.

[13] Birnbaum, A. S. et al. (2002). *Health Education & Behavior, 29,* 427.

[14] Langer, J. A. (2001). *American Educational Research Journal, 38,* 837.

[15] Epstein, M. L., & Brosvic, G. M. (2002) *Psychological Reports, 90,* 1136.

[16] Kim, B. S. K., & Atkinson, D. R. (2002). *Journal of Counseling Psychology, 49,* 3.

[17] Fitzpatrick, M. P., Chapman, G. E., & Barr, S. I. (1997). *Journal of the American Dietetic Association, 97,* 510.

[18] Astleitner, H. (2001). *Journal of Instructional Psychology, 28,* 209.

[19] Czubaj, C. A. (2002). *Education, 122,* 615.

[20] Wells, G. L. (2001). *Psychology, Public Policy, and Law, 7,* 791.

Part B

Directions: Examine several academic journals that publish on topics of interest to you. Identify two with titles you think are especially strong in terms of the evaluation questions presented in this chapter. Also, identify two titles that clearly have weaknesses. Bring the four titles to class for discussion.

Notes

Chapter 3

Evaluating Abstracts

An abstract is a summary of a research report that appears below its title. Like the title, it helps readers identify articles of interest. This function of abstracts is so important that the major computerized databases in the social and behavioral sciences provide abstracts as well as the titles of the articles they index.

Many journals have a policy on the maximum length of abstracts. It is common to allow a maximum of about 100 to 250 words.[1] When evaluating abstracts, you will need to make subjective decisions about how much weight should be given to the various elements that might be included, given that their length typically is severely restricted.

Make a preliminary evaluation of an abstract when you first encounter it. After reading the associated article, reevaluate the abstract. The evaluation questions below are stated as "yes–no" questions, where a "yes" indicates that you judge the characteristic being considered as satisfactory. You may also want to rate each characteristic using a scale from 1 to 5, where 5 is the highest rating. N/A (not applicable) and I/I (insufficient information to make a judgment) may also be used when necessary.

____ 1. Is the purpose of the study referred to or at least clearly implied?

Very satisfactory 5 4 3 2 1 Very unsatisfactory *or* N/A I/I

Comment: Many writers begin their abstracts with a brief statement of the purpose of their research. Examples 3.1.1 and 3.1.2 show the beginnings of abstracts in which this was done. Note that even though the word "purpose" is not used in Example 3.1.2, it is safe to infer that the purpose was to identify the factors that teachers-in-training (i.e., preservice teachers) perceive as barriers to implementing multicultural curriculum.

---

[1] The *Publication Manual of the American Psychological Association* suggests that an abstract should not exceed 120 words. A small number of journals require much more extensive abstracts broken down with subheadings such as *Background*, *Purpose*, *Method*, and so on. These might take up to half a page. Although they are called abstracts, they are similar to executive summaries used in business, which allow busy executives to keep abreast of large numbers of reports coming across their desks without having to read each one in full. Most of the journals that require long, detailed abstracts are in the fields of business and health care.

Example 3.1.1[2]
Beginning of an abstract that describes the purpose of the study:

The purpose of this study was to investigate the relationship of depression to health risk behaviors and health perceptions of Korean college students. The sample consisted....

Example 3.1.2[3]
Beginning of an abstract that implies the purpose of the study:

This study investigated preservice teachers' perceived barriers for implementing multicultural curriculum....

Beginning an abstract with an explicit statement of the research purpose is not necessary if the purpose can be inferred from the title and other information contained in the abstract. Consider the title and beginning of the abstract shown in Example 3.1.3. Taken in their entirety, the title and abstract together make it easy to infer that the purpose is to explore the conditions under which students will yield to peer pressure to ride with an intoxicated driver.

Example 3.1.3[4]
A title and complete abstract that clearly imply the purpose of the study:

Title of an article: The Role of Peer Conformity in the Decision to Ride with an Intoxicated Driver

The associated abstract: Forty university students participated in a study in which they were faced with the decision of whether or not to enter an automobile with an apparently intoxicated driver. Participants were randomly assigned to one of four conditions: driver with one beer, intoxicated driver, intoxicated driver and confederate[5] who enters the car, and intoxicated driver and confederate who refuses to enter the car. Students' decisions whether to enter the car and their concern about the driver's drinking were assessed. Results revealed that participants consistently chose to enter the car in all conditions except when the confederate refused. Condition had no effect on participants' reported concern.

---

[2] Kim, O. (2002). The relationship of depression to health risk behaviors and health perceptions in Korean college students. *Adolescence, 37*, 575–583.

[3] Van Hook, C. W. (2002). Preservice teachers' perceived barriers to the implementation of a multicultural curriculum. *Journal of Instructional Psychology, 29*, 254–264.

[4] Powell, J. L., & Drucker, A. D. (1997). *Journal of Alcohol and Drug Education, 43*, 1–7.

[5] In research, a "confederate" is someone who is posing as a participant in research but in reality is working for the researcher. In this study, the confederate was posing as just another student, when in fact, he or she was working for the researcher.

___ 2. Does the abstract highlight the research methodology?

Very satisfactory   5   4   3   2   1   Very unsatisfactory   *or*   N/A   I/I

Comment: Given the shortness of an abstract, researchers usually can provide only limited details on their methodology. However, even a brief highlight can be helpful to readers who are searching for research reports of interest. Consider Example 3.2.1, which is taken from an abstract. The fact that 400 adults were surveyed by telephone sets it apart from other studies such as those in which adults are mailed questionnaires.

Example 3.2.1[6]
Excerpt from an abstract that mentions methodology:

A telephone survey was administered to 400 adults in the Twin Cities area in Minnesota. The number....

Likewise, the information in Example 3.2.2 provides important information about the researchers' methodology since longitudinal studies (studies of participants over an extended period of time) are relatively rare. Even rarer is the use of students as coresearchers in academic research. These features of the methodology are certainly worth mentioning in an abstract because they clearly distinguish this research article from others on the same general topic.

Example 3.2.2[7]
Excerpt from an abstract that mentions methodology:

The research was part of a six-year longitudinal study of student motivation in which students participated as coresearchers.

___ 3. Has the researcher omitted the titles of measures (except when these are the focus of the research)?

Very satisfactory   5   4   3   2   1   Very unsatisfactory   *or*   N/A   I/I

Comment: Including the full, formal titles of published measures such as tests, questionnaires, and scales in an abstract is *usually* inappropriate (see the exception below) because their names take up space that could be used to convey more important information.[8] Example 3.3.1 illustrates this problem. It

---

[6] Keenan, D. P., AbuSabha, R., & Robinson, N. G. (2002). Consumers' understanding of the Dietary Guidelines for Americans: Insights into the future. *Health Education & Behavior, 29*, 124–135.

[7] Oldfather, P., & Thomas, S. (1998). What does it mean when high school teachers participate in collaborative research with students on literacy motivations? *Teachers College Record, 99*, 647–691.

[8] Note that in many of the social and behavioral sciences, the generic terms "instrument" and "instrumentation" are often used to refer to measures such as tests, scales, interview questions, etc.

is patterned on a portion of an abstract that recently appeared in a leading journal. Example 3.3.2 illustrates how this flaw could have been avoided.

Example 3.3.1
The portion of an abstract dealing with measurement (inappropriate):

A sample of 483 college males completed the Attitudes Toward Alcohol (Fourth Edition, Revised), the Alcohol Use Questionnaire, and the Manns-Herschfield Quantitative Inventory of Alcohol Dependence (Brief Form).

Example 3.3.2
An improved version of Example 3.3.1:

A sample of 483 college males completed measures of their attitudes toward alcohol, their alcohol use, and their dependence on alcohol.

The exception: If the primary purpose of the research is to evaluate the reliability and validity of one or more specific measures, it would be appropriate to name them in the abstract as well as in the title. This will help readers who are interested in learning about the characteristics of specific measures locate relevant research reports. In Example 3.3.3, mentioning the name of a specific measure is appropriate because the focus of the research is the measure.

Example 3.3.3
The portion of an abstract dealing with measurement (appropriate because the purpose of the research is to investigate the measure):

The purpose of the study was to estimate the validity and reliability of the Atkinson Political Activism Scale (Full Scale) as well as the Brief Form of the same scale.

___ 4. Are the highlights of the results described?

Very satisfactory 5 4 3 2 1 Very unsatisfactory *or* N/A I/I

Comment: The last two sentences in Example 3.4.1 describe the highlights of the results of a study, which is appropriate in an abstract. Notice that the researchers state that incompatibility and lack of emotional support were the *most frequently* cited determinants of divorce. However, they do *not* state how frequently these determinants were cited and what other determinants were cited by the women in the study. In other words, they are reporting only highlights.

Example 3.4.1[9]

A complete abstract with highlights of results reported:

Previous research suggests women's reported causes of divorce vary depending on their SES.[10] However, SES has been routinely defined by husbands' income rather than by the women's personal SES. Further, the importance of spousal career support as a determinant of divorce for women has been examined only for highly educated professional women. Utilizing a questionnaire designed for this study, 130 divorced women provided retrospective accounts of factors that led to their divorce. Regardless of women's SES, incompatibility and lack of emotional support were the most frequently cited determinants of divorce. Women divorced fewer than 10 years rated lack of career support as a more important factor in their divorce than did women who had been divorced for a longer time.

Note that there is nothing inherently wrong with giving specific results (and statistics) if space permits and if they are not misleading out of the context of the full research report. Example 3.4.2 illustrates this. First, the researcher notes that three themes "predominated," which suggests a majority noted these themes. Then there is mention of a specific statistic: "one-third." Notice, however, that the author still is citing only highlights, for example, by using the phrase "by at least one-third" rather than stating the specific fraction (or associated percentage) for each of the three additional themes.

Example 3.4.2[11]

Part of an abstract with some specific results reported as highlights:

Interviews with a diverse group of juniors and seniors from three secondary schools in the northeastern United States revealed substantial agreement in their images of America. Three themes predominated: inequality associated with race, gender, socioeconomic status, or disability; freedom including rights and opportunities; and diversity based on race, ethnicity, culture, and geography. Three additional themes were voiced by at least one-third of the students: America as better than other nations, progress, and the American dream. Crosscutting these themes were a sense of individualism or personalization and....

---

[9] Dolan, M. A., & Hoffman, C. D. (1998). Determinants of divorce among women: A reexamination of critical influences. *Journal of Divorce and Remarriage, 28*, 97–106.

[10] SES stands for socioeconomic status.

[11] Cornbleth, C. (2002). Images of America: What youth *do* know about the United States. *American Educational Research Journal, 39*, 519–552.

___ 5. If the study is strongly tied to a theory, is the theory mentioned in the abstract?

Very satisfactory   5   4   3   2   1   Very unsatisfactory   *or*   N/A   I/I

Comment: As you know from the last chapter, a theory that is central to a study might be mentioned in the title. If such a theory is not mentioned in the title, it should be mentioned in the abstract, as illustrated in Example 3.5.1 It is also acceptable to mention it in both the title and abstract, as illustrated in Example 3.5.2. (Note that bold italics have been used in these examples for emphasis.)

Example 3.5.1[12]

Title and abstract in which a specific theory is mentioned in the abstract but not the title (acceptable to deemphasize theory):

Title: College-Educated Women's Personality Development in Adulthood Perceptions and Age Differences

Abstract: Adulthood encompasses a large time span and includes a series of psychosocial challenges (E. H. Erikson, 1950). Five aspects of personality (identity certainty, confident power, concern with aging, generativity, and personal distress) were assessed in a cross-sectional study of college-educated women who at the time of data collection were young adults (age: $M = 26$ years), middle-aged adults (age: $M = 46$ years), or older adults (age: $M = 66$ years). Respondents rated each personality domain for how true it was of them at the time, and they then rated the other two ages either retrospectively or prospectively. Results are discussed with attention to the ways in which women's adult development may have been shaped by experiences particular to both gender and birth cohort, and to how these women fit with ***E. H. Erikson's theory of adult development***.

Example 3.5.2[13]

Title and abstract in which a specific theory is mentioned in the title and abstract (acceptable to emphasize theory):

Title: Testing ***Self-Focused Attention Theory*** in Clinical Supervision Effects on Supervisee Anxiety and Performance

Abstract: Audio- or videotaping and one-way mirrors are often used in clinical supervision. Yet, the effects of audio- or videotaping on supervisees have yielded equivocal results. Some studies suggest that audio- or videotaping increases trainee anxiety and hinders performance, whereas other studies suggest negligible effects. The authors present two studies in which they tested ***self-focused attention theory*** (e.g., C. S. Carver & M. F. Scheier, 1982; S. Duval & R. A. Wicklund, 1972) to explain the equivocal findings. In each study, trainees were randomly assigned to one of three awareness conditions (private or public

---

[12]Zucker, A. N., Ostrove, J. M., & Stewart, A. J. (2002). *Psychology and Aging, 17*, 236–244.
[13]Ellis, M. V., Krengel, M., & Beck, M. (2002). *Journal of Counseling Psychology, 49*, 101–116.

self-awareness, or subjective awareness) and conducted initial counseling sessions. Analyses of supervisee anxiety and performance found no significant differences due to self-awareness condition in either study. The results suggest that a mirror and audio- or videotaping elicit trivial aversive effects on supervisees.

___ 6. Has the researcher avoided making vague references to implications and future research directions?

Very satisfactory 5 4 3 2 1 Very unsatisfactory *or* N/A I/I

Comment: Most researchers discuss the implications of their research and directions for future research near the end of their research reports. However, the limited amount of space allotted to abstracts should not be used to make vague references to these matters. Example 3.6.1 is the closing sentence from an abstract. It contains vague references to implications and future research.

Example 3.6.1
Last sentence of an abstract with vague references to implications and future research (inappropriate):

This article concludes with a discussion of both the implications of the results and directions for future research.

Example 3.6.1 could safely be omitted from the abstract without causing a loss of important information because most readers will correctly assume that most research reports discuss these elements. An alternative to omitting it is to state something specific about these matters, as illustrated in Example 3.6.2. Notice that in this example, the researcher does not describe the implications but tells us something specific: The implications will be of special interest to a particular group of professionals—school counselors. This will alert school counselors that this research report (among the many hundreds of others on drug abuse) might be of special interest to them. If space does not permit such a long closing sentence in the abstract, it could be shortened to "Implications for school counselors are discussed."[14]

Example 3.6.2
Improved version of Example 3.6.1 (last sentence of an abstract):

While these results have implications for all professionals who work with

---

[14] Note that this statement would not be needed if it appeared in an abstract in a journal with a title such as *Research in School Counseling*, because it would be reasonable to expect that all research reports in such a journal would contain discussions of implications for school counselors. Hence, it is not necessary to refer to implications in an abstract unless the researcher can say something about the implications that adds information and helps consumers of research locate articles appropriate to their interests.

adolescents who abuse drugs, special attention is given to the implications for school counselors.

In short, implications and future research do not necessarily need to be mentioned in abstracts. If they are mentioned, however, something specific should be said about them.

___ **7. Overall, is the abstract effective and appropriate?**

Very satisfactory 5 4 3 2 1 Very unsatisfactory *or* N/A I/I

Comment: Rate this evaluation question after considering your answers to the earlier ones in this chapter and any additional considerations and concerns you may have. Be prepared to rewrite the abstracts of research reports to which you assign low ratings.

Exercise for Chapter 3

Part A

Directions: Evaluate each of the following abstracts (to the extent that it is possible to do so without reading the associated articles) by answering Evaluation Question 7 (Overall, is the abstract effective and appropriate?) using a scale from 1 (poor) to 5 (excellent). In the explanations for your ratings, refer to the other six evaluation questions in this chapter.

References for the following abstracts are given in the footnotes. The journals in which they appeared are widely available in large academic libraries, making it possible for you to consult the complete articles if they are assigned by your instructor. More definitive application of the evaluation criteria for abstracts is possible by first reading complete articles and then evaluating their abstracts.

1. *Title*: An Investigation into the Relationship Between Effective Administrative Leadership Styles and the Use of Technology[15]

   Abstract: Advances in technology have inspired a growing debate regarding effective instructional strategies in our present educational system. As the roles and responsibilities of administrative leaders shift, this research was conducted to ascertain what leadership attributes affect the integration of technology to improve teaching and learning. A survey of Ohio public educators was conducted to identify faculty perceptions of building leadership and how these perceptions influence attitudes toward innovative technology implementation

---

[15] Hughes, M., & Zachariah, S. (2001). *International Electronic Journal for Leadership in Learning, 5.* Retrieved from http://www.acs.ucalgary.ca/~iejll/ on December 15, 2002.

efforts, and ultimately student achievement. This study focuses on the relationship between administrative leadership styles and implementation of new technological programs or instructional strategies.

Overall, is the abstract effective and appropriate?
5   4   3   2   1

Explain your rating:

2. *Title*: Educational Status of Children Who Are Receiving Services in an Urban Family Preservation and Reunification Setting[16]

Abstract: Examines the educational performance of children who are receiving services from an urban child care service agency, with an emphasis on family preservation and reunification. Participants for the study were 56 children (30 boys and 26 girls), ranging from 1st to 8th grade or between ages 6 and 15. Information on the educational performance of the participants was collected using the Educational Status Form, a 14-item questionnaire. Data included educational performance, attendance pattern, and family status. The majority of the study participants were performing poorly in core academic areas. In addition, the students averaged 16 days absent and almost 9 days tardy. Twenty-five percent of the participants had already repeated one or more grades. No relationships were reported between school performance and family status. The results of the study, limitations, future research needs, and the need for early intervention are discussed.

Overall, is the abstract effective and appropriate?
5   4   3   2   1

Explain your rating:

3. *Title*: Wrong Side of the Tracks: Exploring the Role of Newspaper Coverage of Homicide in Socially Constructing Dangerous Places[17]

Abstract: While much research has been conducted concerning the coverage of crime by the media, little is known about the spatial aspect of this coverage. Specifically, media research has failed to determine whether the coverage of crime by the media is truly representative of where crime occurs, or whether media coverage presents crime as occurring disproportionately in certain areas of a city. Building on earlier research, and utilizing an exhaustive spatial data set and advanced spatial statistics, this research attempts to determine the degree to which newspaper coverage of homicide is spatially representative of the true homicide picture. Findings indicate that actual homicide hot spots near the city center are more likely to be covered than those on the periphery of the city and that celebrated news

---

[16] Epstein, M. H. et. al. (1998). *Journal of Emotional and Behavioral Disorders, 6,* 162–169.
[17] Paulsen. D. J. (2002). *Journal of Criminal Justice and Popular Culture, 9,* 113–127.

coverage is focused largely within the city center. In addition to trends in the spatial coverage of homicides, important social implications relating to fear of crime will be discussed.

Overall, is the abstract effective and appropriate?
5   4   3   2   1

Explain your rating:

4.   *Title*: Eating Disorder Symptomatology and Substance Use in College Females[18]

Abstract: The purpose of this study was to examine the relationship between eating disorder symptomatology and substance use (i.e., marijuana, nicotine, cocaine, amphetamines, diet pills, tranquilizers, psychedelics) in a female college student population. A sample of 195 female college students (aged 17–25 yrs) completed the Eating Disorder Inventory, the Quantitative Inventory of Alcohol Disorders, and the Demographic and Drug Use Questionnaire. An insignificant relationship between substance use and eating disorder symptomatology was found. Despite this lack of relationship, relatively high levels of eating disorder symptomatology and problematic alcohol use were found. Implications for college professionals are discussed.

Overall, is the abstract effective and appropriate?
5   4   3   2   1

Explain your rating:

5.   *Title*: Psychological Reactions to Redress: Diversity Among Japanese Americans Interned During World War II[19]

Abstract: The psychological reactions of 2nd-generation (Nisei) Japanese Americans to receiving redress from the U.S. government for the injustices of their World War II internment were investigated. The respondents, all of whom had been interned during the war, rated the degree to which the receipt of redress nearly 50 years after their incarceration was associated with eight different areas of personal impact. Results indicated that redress was reported to be most effective in increasing faith in the government and least effective in reducing physical suffering from the internment. Women and older respondents reported more positive redress effects. In addition, lower levels of current income, an attitudinal preference for Japanese Americans, and preredress support for seeking monetary compensation each increased the prediction of positive redress effects. Findings are discussed in relation to theories of social and retributive justice.

Overall, is the abstract effective and appropriate?
5   4   3   2   1

Explain your rating:

[18] Kashubeck, S., & Mintz, L. B. (1996). *Journal of College Student Development, 37*, 396–404.
[19] Nagata, D. K., & Takeshita, Y. J. (2002). *Cultural Diversity and Ethnic Minority Psychology, 8*, 41–59.

6. *Title*: Changes Over Time in Teenage Sexual Relationships: Comparing the High School Class of 1950, 1975, and 2000[20]

Abstract: This study investigated the sexual attitudes and experiences in adolescence of 242 individuals who graduated from the same high school in the northeastern United States over a 50-year period. Specifically, a survey was mailed to members of the class of 1950, the class of 1975, and the class of 2000 to examine changes over time. Overall findings suggest a significant change in sexual attitudes and experiences when comparing the class of 1950 to the classes of 1975 and 2000.

Overall, is the abstract effective and appropriate?
5   4   3   2   1

Explain your rating:

7. *Title*: Development and Validation of a Modified Version of the Peritraumatic Dissociative Experiences Questionnaire [21]

Abstract: This article reports results from three studies conducted to develop and validate a modified version of the self-administered form of the Peritraumatic Dissociative Experiences Questionnaire (PDEQ; C. R. Marmar, D. S. Weiss, & T. J. Metzler, 1997). The objective was to develop an instrument suitable for use with persons from diverse ethnic and socioeconomic backgrounds. In Study 1, the original PDEQ was administered to a small sample ($N = 15$) recruited from among men admitted to the hospital for physical injuries stemming from exposure to community violence. Results led to modifications aimed at improving the utility of the instrument. In Study 2, the modified PDEQ was subjected to structural equation modeling and item response theory analyses to assess its psychometric properties in a larger, primarily male, sample of community violence survivors ($N = 284$). In Study 3, the reliability and validity of the modified instrument were further assessed in a sample of female survivors of sexual assault ($N = 90$). Results attest to the psychometric properties as well as the reliability and validity of the modified 8-item PDEQ.

Overall, is the abstract effective and appropriate?
5   4   3   2   1

Explain your rating:

---

[20] Caron, S. L., & Moskey, E. G. (2002). *Adolescence, 37*, 515–526.
[21] Marshall, G. N., Orlando, M., Jaycox, L. H., Foy, D. W., & Belzberg, H. (2002). *Psychological Assessment, 14*, 123–134.

Part B

Directions: Examine several academic journals that publish on topics of interest to you. Identify two with abstracts that you think are especially strong in terms of the evaluation questions presented in this chapter. Also, identify two abstracts that clearly have weaknesses. Bring the four abstracts to class for discussion.

Chapter 4

Evaluating Introductions and Literature Reviews

Research reports in academic journals almost always begin with an introduction in which literature is cited.[1] An integrated introduction and literature review has these five purposes: (a) introduce the problem area, (b) establish its importance, (c) provide an overview of the relevant literature, (d) show how the current study will advance knowledge in the area, and (e) describe the researcher's specific research questions, purposes, or hypotheses, which usually are stated in the last paragraph of the introduction.

This chapter presents evaluation questions regarding the introduction. In the next chapter, the selection and presentation of the literature will be examined more closely.

____ 1. Does the researcher begin by identifying a specific problem area?

Very satisfactory 5 4 3 2 1 Very unsatisfactory *or* N/A I/I

Comment: Some researchers start their introductions with statements that are so broad they fail to identify the specific area for investigation. As the beginning of an introduction to a study on the effects of smoking and obesity, Example 4.1.1 is deficient. Notice that it fails to identify the specific areas of public health that are explored in the research.

Example 4.1.1
Beginning of an inappropriately broad introduction:

State and local governments expend considerable resources for research on public health issues. The findings of this research are used to formulate public policies that regulate health-related activities within the broader society. In addition to helping establish regulations, public health agencies attempt to educate the public so that individuals have appropriate information when making individual lifestyle decisions that may affect their health.

---

[1] In theses and dissertations, the first chapter usually is an introduction, with relatively few references to the literature. This is followed by a chapter that provides a comprehensive literature review.

Example 4.1.2 illustrates a more appropriate beginning for a research report on public health issues—in this case, the relative risks of smoking and obesity to health.

Example 4.1.2[2]

A specific beginning. (Compare with Example 4.1.1.):

Cigarette smoking and obesity are both widespread and significant health liabilities that increase the risks of hypertension, ischemic heart disease, noninsulin-dependent diabetes, and various types of cancer. Objectively, the relative risks associated with smoking outstrip those associated with obesity (U.S. Department of Health and Human Services, 1990). At most weight levels, smokers suffer nearly twice the mortality of nonsmokers from cancer, heart disease, stroke, and diabetes (VanItallie, 1992). The mortality associated with being overweight approaches the mortality associated with smoking only when weight exceeds 110% of desirable, healthy body weight (Hahn, Teutsch, Rothenberg, & Marks, 1990; VanItallie, 1992).

Making a decision as to whether a researcher has started the introduction by being reasonably specific often involves some subjectivity. As a general rule, the researcher should get to the point quickly without using valuable journal space to outline a very broad problem area rather than the specific one(s) that he or she has directly studied.

___ 2. Does the researcher establish the importance of the problem area?

Very satisfactory 5 4 3 2 1 Very unsatisfactory *or* N/A I/I

Comment: Researchers select research problems they believe are important, and they should specifically address this belief early in their introductions. Often, this is done by citing previously published statistics that indicate how widespread a problem is, how many people are affected by it, and so on. Example 4.2.1 illustrates how one researcher did this in the first paragraph of a study on the effectiveness of an educational program for incarcerated adults with disabilities. Note that there are many hundreds of studies on incarceration (numbers who are incarcerated, ethnicity of the incarcerated, effects of various forms of punishment, legal issues regarding incarceration, ethical and political issues regarding capital punishment, and so on). However, the authors of

---

[2] Johnsen, L., Spring, B., Pingitore, R., Sommerfeld, B. K., & MacKirnan, D. (2002). Smoking as subculture? Influence on Hispanic and non-Hispanic White women's attitudes toward smoking and obesity. *Health Psychology, 21*, 279–287.

Example 4.2.1 avoid muddling their introduction with information on numerous, potentially related issues. Instead, they focus immediately on academic achievement and the disabled, citing specific statistics (e.g., "only half" and "two-thirds") to justify their study.

Example 4.2.1[3]

First paragraph of an introduction that includes statistics to establish the importance of a problem area:

Accumulating evidence suggests that low academic achievement is a major factor in crime (Farnworth & Leiber, 1989; Williamson, 1992). According to the Bureau of Justice Statistics (2000), only half of the inmates in federal, state, or local jails have a high school diploma or its equivalent, a third have a mental or physical disability, and almost two-thirds were unemployed during the month before their arrest. Research also shows that inmates with special education needs are overrepresented in juvenile and adult correctional facilities (Fink, 1990; Rutherford, Nelson, & Wolford, 1985; Morgan, 1979; Winters, 1997). The disproportionate number of students with an emotional or learning disability who drop out of school most likely adds to these numbers (Phelps & Hanley-Maxwell, 1997).

Example 4.2.2 also uses statistical information (rank of cause of death) to justify the importance of examining variables associated with suicide among African American women. Note that instead of beginning with a general discussion of suicide in the United States, the researchers focus immediately on the group they studied (i.e., African American women who attempted suicide). Also notice the citation from a prominent government agency that is widely respected for its collection of public health statistics (i.e., the Centers for Disease Control and Prevention).

Example 4.2.2[4]

Beginning of an introduction that includes statistical information to establish the importance of a problem area:

Suicide is a significant public health problem among African American women in the United States. Mortality data indicate that suicide was the fifth leading cause of death among 15–19-year-old, the seventh leading

---

[3] Bottge, B. A., & Watson, E. A. (2002). Using video-based math problems to connect the skills and understandings of incarcerated adults with disabilities. *Journal of Special Education Technology, 17.* No page numbers given. The example appears on the first page of this URL, which is maintained by the journal: http://jset.unlv.edu/17.2/bottge/first.html. Retrieved December 12, 2002.

[4] Thompson, M. P., Kaslow, N. J., Short, L. M., & Wyckoff, S. (2002). The mediating roles of perceived social support and resources in the self-efficacy-suicide attempts relation among African American abused women. *Journal of Consulting and Clinical Psychology, 70,* 942–949.

cause of death among 10–14- and 20–24-year-old, and the ninth leading cause of death among 25–34-year-old African American women and girls in 1997 (Centers for Disease Control and Prevention, 1999).

Because one of the most significant risk factors for suicide completions is a previous suicide attempt (Maris, Burnam, Maltsberger, & Yufit, 1992), identifying risk factors for suicide attempts can potentially reduce this public health burden. One identified risk factor for suicide attempts among women in general (Abbott, Johnson, Koziol-McLain, & Lowenstein, 1995; Amaro, Fried, Cabral, & Zuckerman, 1990; Bergman & Brismar, 1991; Kaplan, Asnis, Lipschitz, & Chorney, 1995; Roberts, Lawrence, O'Toole, & Raphael, 1997), and among African American women specifically (Kaslow et al., 1998; Stark & Flitcraft, 1996), is intimate partner violence. Intimate partner violence has been found to more than double the risk of suicide attempts among African American women (Kaslow et al., 1998).

Not all women who are exposed to intimate partner violence make suicide attempts. Unfortunately, little research has examined....

Instead of providing statistics on the prevalence of problems, researchers sometimes use other strategies to convince readers of the importance of the research problems they studied. One approach is to show that a topic is of current interest because of corporate or government actions, such as the passage of the Americans with Disabilities Act. Another is to show that prominent people or influential authors have considered and addressed the issue that is being researched. Example 4.2.3 is the beginning of an article that illustrates the latter technique. The names of influential people in the example are italicized and put in bold here for emphasis. Also note that showing there has been an interest in the topic dating back centuries also helps to establish the importance of the problem. Providing a historical content to introduce a problem will be discussed again in the next chapter.

Example 4.2.3[5]

Excerpt from the beginning of an introduction that uses a nonstatistical argument to establish the importance of a problem:

Since at least the sixth century B.C., happiness has been considered a primary and necessary component of *eudaimonia* or the worthwhile life (Taylor, 1998). Living well is a combination of both a favorable objective evaluation of one's situation (i.e., reasoned) and a favorable subjective assessment of one's well-being (i.e., felt). Today, this belief continues, though with a clearly greater emphasis on just the latter, subjective well-

---

[5] Steel, P., & Ones, D. S. (2002). Personality and happiness: A national-level analysis. *Journal of Personality and Social Psychology, 83,* 767–781.

being (SWB) part. In reflection of this importance, a considerable amount of research has been conducted on topics ranging from job satisfaction (e.g., Judge, Bono, & Locke, 2000) to life satisfaction (e.g.,Veenhoven, 1996), as well as considering the links between the two (e.g., Ernst & Ozeki, 1998). The total number of articles dealing with individual SWB is so large that almost 10,000 studies and almost 60 separate meta-analyses have been conducted involving happiness at work alone (i.e., job satisfaction; Judge & Bono, 2001).

In addition to our fascination with individual-level happiness, we have become especially interested in the last few hundred years in determining what makes the group happy too. Influential thinkers such as *Jeremy Bentham* and *John Stuart Mill* have argued that we should seek the greatest good for the greatest number. In a similar vein, Murray (1988) traces the adoption of happiness as the ultimate goal for government, quoting notable American historical figures such as *James Madison*, *John Adams*, and *George Washington*. Such is its acceptance that the United States' Declaration of Independence has the sentiment enshrined: "We hold these truths to be self-evident, that all men are created equal, that they are endowed by their Creator with certain unalienable Rights, that among these are Life, Liberty and *the pursuit of Happiness* [italics added]."

Finally, a researcher may attempt to establish the nature and importance of a problem by citing anecdotal evidence or personal experience. While this is arguably the weakest way to establish the importance of a problem, a unique and interesting anecdote might convince readers that the problem is important enough to investigate.

A caveat: When you apply Evaluation Question 2 to the introduction of a research report, do *not* confuse the importance of a problem with your personal interest in the problem. It is possible to have little personal interest in a problem yet still recognize that a researcher has established its importance. On the other hand, it is possible to have a strong personal interest in a problem but judge that the researcher has failed to make a strong argument (or has failed to present convincing evidence) to establish its importance.

____ 3. Are any underlying theories adequately described?

Very satisfactory 5 4 3 2 1 Very unsatisfactory *or* N/A I/I

Comment: Much useful research is *nontheoretical*. Sometimes the purpose of a study is simply to collect and interpret data in order to make a practical decision. For instance, a researcher might poll parents to determine what percentage favors a proposed new regulation that would require students to wear uniforms when attending school. Nontheoretical information on parents' attitudes toward requiring uniforms might be an important consideration when a school board is making a decision on the issue.

Another major reason for conducting nontheoretical research is to determine whether there is a problem and/or the incidence of the problem. For instance, a researcher might collect data on the percentage of pregnant women using county medical services who use tobacco products during pregnancy and the amounts they use. The resulting data will help decision makers determine how important this problem is within the population to which they are providing medical treatment, which would have implications for the allocation of resources for dealing with this problem. Of course, other researchers might conduct research on theories that might help explain why some pregnant women engage in such a risky health-related behavior. While theoretical research might help explain many different types of risky health-related behaviors, it might also contribute to understanding the particular behavior in question (smoking by pregnant women) and have implications for which treatments to use to reduce its incidence.

When applying Evaluation Question 3 to nontheoretical research, "not applicable" (N/A) will usually be the best answer. However, if a theory is alluded to or specifically named in the introduction to a research article, the theory or theories should be adequately described. Deciding whether it is adequately described can be highly subjective because well-known theories need not be described in great detail while newer, emerging theories should be described in much greater detail. As a general rule, even a well-known theory should be described in at least a short paragraph (along with one or more references where additional information can be found) for readers who may be new to the field. Note that if the explicit, stated purpose of research is to test a proposition or prediction based on a theory, one would expect the theory to be discussed in detail even if it is well known.

Example 4.3.1 briefly but clearly summarizes the theory of planned behavior (TPB), which is well known, especially among those who conduct health-related research. Even though the purpose of the study was to test the applicability of the theory to understanding the behavior of individuals in a very specific population (individuals in cardiac rehabilitation) on a specific outcome (compliance in following an exercise regime), the theory is first described in general terms, followed by a citation to a reference where more information on the theory can be found.[6] Whether Example 4.3.1 describes the theory accurately is a matter that would need to be considered by experts on the theory. However, consumers of research can easily make a judgment as to

---

[6] Particular aspects of the theory in relation to the variables being studied are discussed in great detail in subsequent portions of the article.

whether the description is adequate in terms of specificity and clarity of presentation.

Example 4.3.1[7]

Paragraph from the introduction to a research article that describes a theory that underlies the research:

The TPB [Theory of Planned Behavior] proposes that a person's intention to perform a behavior is the major determinant of that behavior. Furthermore, a person's intention is determined by three theoretically independent variables: (a) a person's attitude, which is indicated by a positive or negative evaluation of performing the behavior; (b) subjective norm, the perceived social pressure that individuals may feel to perform or not perform the behavior; (c) perceived behavioral control (PBC), the perceived ease or difficulty of performing the behavior, which may have both direct and indirect effects on behavior. The TPB proposes that individuals will intend to perform a behavior when they evaluate it positively, believe that important others think they should perform it, and perceive it to be under their control (Ajzen, 1991).

A special note for evaluating qualitative research: Often, qualitative researchers explore problem areas without initial reference to theory and hypotheses based on it. Instead, they develop theories (and models and other generalizations) as they collect and analyze data. The data often take the form of transcripts from open-ended interviews, notes on direct observation and participation in activities with participants, and so on. Thus, in a research article reporting on qualitative research, a theory might not be described until the results and discussion section (instead of the introduction). When this is the case, apply Evaluation Question 3 at the point at which theory is discussed.

___ 4. Does the introduction move from topic to topic instead of from citation to citation?

Very satisfactory   5   4   3   2   1   Very unsatisfactory   *or*   N/A   I/I

Comment: Introductions that typically fail on this evaluation question are organized around citations rather than topics. For example, a researcher might inappropriately first summarize Smith's study, then summarize Jones' study, then summarize Doe's study, and so on. The result is a series of annotations that are merely strung together. This fails to guide readers through the literature and

---

[7] Blanchard, C. M., Courneya, K. S., Rodgers, W. M., Daub, B., & Knapik, G. (2002). Determinants of exercise intention and behavior during and after phase 2 cardiac rehabilitation: An application of the Theory of Planned Behavior. *Rehabilitation Psychology, 47*, 308–323.

fails to show how the various references relate to each other and what they mean as a whole.

In contrast, an introduction should be organized around topics and subtopics with references cited as needed, often in groups of two or more citations to literature. For example, if four research reports support a certain point, the point usually should be stated with all four references cited together. This was done in the third sentence of Example 4.2.1 above, in which there are four references given to support a single finding: that inmates with special needs are overrepresented in correctional facilities.

In Example 4.4.1 below, there are two citations to *reviews* of literature to support the beneficial effects of regular exercise. Presumably, reviews are potentially more valid sources because they represent a body of findings—not just the findings of individual studies. Also note that there are two other groups of two citations (cited together within parentheses) within the example, such as the one in the last sentence.

Example 4.4.1[8]

An excerpt from a literature review with references cited in groups:

Research indicates that regular exercise has favorable effects on mental health, self-esteem, and sense of overall well-being (see U.S. Department of Health and Human Services, 1996; Morgan, 1997, for reviews). It has been cited as useful for treating psychological disorders such as depression (Craft & Landers, 1998) and anxiety (Martinsen, 1993; Landers & Petruzzello, 1994), as well as providing prophylactic effects (Plante, 1993). Exercise improves psychological states in individuals already within "normal" ranges; however, those with the most unfavorable emotional states may benefit most (North, McCullah, & Tran, 1990; Petruzzello, Landers, Hatfield, Kubitz, & Salazar, 1991).

Of course, when a researcher is discussing a reference that is crucial to a point he or she is making, that reference should be discussed in more detail than was done in Example 4.4.1. However, because research reports in academic journals are expected to be relatively brief, this should be done sparingly and only for the most important related literature.

___ **5. Is the research a coherent essay with logical transitions from topic to topic?**

Very satisfactory 5 4 3 2 1 Very unsatisfactory *or* N/A I/I

---

[8] Annesi, J. J. (2002). Relation of rated fatigue and changes in energy after exercise and over 14 weeks in previously sedentary women exercisers. *Perceptual and Motor Skills, 95*, 719–727.

Comment: When there are a number of issues to be covered in a long introduction, there may be several essays, each with its own subheading, which help guide readers. Each of the paragraphs normally should have the typical organization with a topic idea (often stated in the first sentence) that is enlarged on and supported by details (usually citations to previous research). Transitions from one paragraph to the next should be logical. Often, researchers do this by starting paragraphs with transitional terms, as illustrated in Example 4.5.1, which deals with the role of the media in shaping public perceptions of the president of the United States.

Example 4.5.1[9]

The beginnings of six paragraphs from an introduction to research. (Paragraphs 2 through 6 begin with transitional terms, which are shown in italics for emphasis.):

Research has shown that news coverage can focus public attention on particular topics and, in so doing, alter the mix of cognitions that are most readily accessible when forming political judgments (Dalton, Beck, and Huckfeldt, 1998…).

Consistent with this work, yet adopting a longitudinal perspective, Pan and Kosicki (1997) suggest that research on public opinion needs to pay closer attention to.…

In particular, economic news coverage—specifically, emphasis upon favorable or unfavorable developments or indicators—may help shape evaluations of presidential job performance because.…

Consistent with this view, Hetherington (1996) found that the quantity of political information consumed by citizens.…

Similarly, research suggests that coverage of a president's general performance on policy issues plays a key role in molding approval ratings (Brody, 1991). Iyengar and colleagues (see Iyengar, 1991; Iyengar and Kinder, 1987) have suggested that news.…

In addition, scholars have distinguished between the private and public aspects of political performance—that is, "between the personal and the presidential" (Jamieson, 1998, p.21; also Lawrence, Bennett, and Hunt, 1999). This distinction suggests that.…

____ 6. Has the researcher provided conceptual definitions of key terms?

Very satisfactory   5   4   3   2   1   Very unsatisfactory   *or*   N/A   I/I

---

[9] Shah, D. V., Watts, M. D., Domke, D., & Fan, D. P. (2002). News framing and cueing of issue regimes: Explaining Clinton's public approval in spite of scandal. *Public Opinion Quarterly*, *66*, 339–370.

Comment: Often, researchers will pause at appropriate points in their introductions to offer formal conceptual definitions,[10] such as the one shown in Example 4.6.1. Note that it is acceptable for a researcher to cite a previously published definition—in this case, one proposed by Rousseau et al.

Example 4.6.1[11]

A conceptual definition provided in an introduction:

Rousseau et al. (1998) proposed the following definition of trust as it has been conceptualized and studied across numerous disciplines: "A psychological state comprising the intention to accept vulnerability based upon positive expectations of the intentions or behavior of another" (p. 395). We use this conceptual definition in our analysis, recognizing that researchers have operationalized it in different ways and for different types of leadership referents (e.g., ranging from direct leader to organizational leadership).

Sometimes important terms are not formally defined, but their meanings are made clear by the context of the introduction. For instance, researchers might cite examples of what is and is not covered by a key term they are using, which helps to define it.

At times, researchers may offer neither formal definitions nor in-context definitions, and you may judge that the terms have such widespread commonly held definitions that they do not need to be defined. For example, in a report of research on various methods of teaching handwriting, a researcher may not offer a definition of handwriting in his or her introduction, and you might judge this to be acceptable. Of course, you will expect the researcher to describe later how handwriting was measured (i.e., the *operational definition*) when you get to the details of the methods used to conduct the research.

In sum, this evaluation question should not be applied mechanically by looking to see if there is a specific statement of a definition. The mere absence of one does not necessarily mean that a researcher has failed on this evaluation question. Instead, you may judge that a definition simply is not needed.

____ 7. Has the researcher indicated the basis for "factual" statements?

Very satisfactory   5   4   3   2   1   Very unsatisfactory   *or*   N/A   I/I

---

[10] A *conceptual definition* seeks to identify a term using only general concepts but with enough specificity that the term is not confused with other related terms or concepts. As such, they resemble dictionary definitions. In contrast, an *operational definition* describes the physical process used to examine a variable.
[11] Dirks, K. T., & Ferrin, D. L. (2002). Trust in leadership: Meta-analytic findings and implications for research and practice. *Journal of Applied Psychology, 87*, 611–628.

Comment: Researchers should avoid making statements that sound like "facts" without referring to their source. As you know from freshman composition, this is highly undesirable. A common statement of this type is the unsubstantiated claim that interest in a problem is growing or that the number of people affected by a problem is increasing, which is illustrated in Example 4.7.1. Notice that not only is the "fact" not substantiated with a reference to its source, it is also vague because "dramatically" is not defined. Example 4.7.2 is an improved version.

Example 4.7.1
An unreferenced "factual" claim:

Interest in child abuse and mistreatment has increased dramatically in recent years.

Example 4.7.2[12]
A referenced "fact." (Compare with Example 4.7.1.):

Child maltreatment incident reports increased by 50% between 1988 and 1993, totaling more than 2.9 million reports in 1993 (McCurdy & Daro, 1994). Much of this increase can be attributed to....

Note, however, that it is appropriate for researchers to express their opinions in introductions as long as the context makes it clear that they are opinions and not "facts." In Example 4.7.3, the researchers express what is clearly an opinion because of their use of the word "presumption."

Example 4.7.3[13]
A statement properly identified as an opinion:

The presumption here is that literacy is context sensitive; that is, varied contexts (economic, cultural, gendered, geographical, historical, ideological, linguistic, racial/ethnic, religious, and social) affect access to literacy and opportunity for its development and use. Given these considerations, equal outcomes should not be expected from unequal circumstances.

___ 8. Do the specific research purposes, questions, or hypotheses logically flow from the introductory material?

Very satisfactory 5 4 3 2 1 Very unsatisfactory *or* N/A I/I

---

[12] Akin, B. A., & Gregoire, T. K. (1997). Parents' views on child welfare's response to addiction. *Families in Society: The Journal of Contemporary Human Services, 78*, 393–404.
[13] Willis, A. I. (2002). Literacy at Calhoun Colored School: 1892–1945. *Reading Research Quarterly, 37*, 8–44.

Comment: Typically, the specific research purposes, questions, or hypotheses that drive a research study are stated in the last paragraph of the introduction.[14] The material preceding them should set the stage and logically lead to them. For example, if a researcher argues that research methods used by previous researchers are not well suited for answering certain research questions, you would not be surprised to learn that his or her research purpose is to reexamine the research questions using alternative research methods. Likewise, if a researcher points out in the introduction that there are certain specific gaps in what is known about a problem area (i.e., the previously published literature has not covered certain subtopics), you would not be surprised to learn that the purpose of the study that is being introduced is designed to fill those gaps. Example 4.8.1 is the last paragraph in the introduction to a research report on adolescents' use of dietary supplements marketed as athletic performance enhancers. In the paragraph, the researchers provide a very brief statement on the literature that they reviewed in the introduction. This sets the stage for the two specific research purposes, which are stated in the last sentence of the example.

Example 4.8.1[15]

Last paragraph of an introduction (beginning with a summary of the research that was reviewed and ending with a statement of the purposes of the current research):

[The] research [reviewed above] has shown that a substantial number of adolescents use dietary supplements, but the factors influencing this behavior are still unclear. However, attitudes and beliefs about the positive aspects of supplement use and the influence of significant others seem to be important factors. The purpose of the present study was (1) to determine whether attitudes are a better predictor of adolescents' intentions to use dietary supplements than are subjective norms and (2) to assess the influence of significant others (coaches, parents, and trainers) on attitudes, subjective norms, and intentions among adolescent athletes.

___ 9. Overall, is the introduction effective and appropriate?

Very satisfactory 5 4 3 2 1 Very unsatisfactory *or* N/A I/I

---

[14] Some researchers state their research purposes, questions, or hypotheses in general terms near the beginning of their introductions and then restate them more specifically near the end.

[15] Dunn, M. S. et al. (2001). The influence of significant others on attitudes, subjective norms, and intentions regarding dietary supplement use among adolescent athletes. *Adolescence, 36,* 583–591.

Comment: Rate this evaluation question after considering your answers to the earlier ones in this chapter and any additional considerations and concerns you may have. Be prepared to explain your overall evaluation.

Exercise for Chapter 4

Part A

Directions: Below is the introduction to a brief research report published in an academic journal.[16] Using the scales that follow the introduction, rate it on the nine evaluation questions in this chapter. Use N/A for "not applicable" and "I/I" for insufficient information to make a rating.

Needle sharing is not only prevalent (Dinwiddie, 1997) but also can occur for many reasons, including historical, legal, economic, or sociocultural factors (DesJarlais, Friedman, & Strug, 1986). Sharing may be due in part to the scarcity of sterile needles or to the economic burden of acquiring sterile needles (Koester & Hoffer, 1994; Mandell, Vlahov, Cohn, Latkin, & Oziemkowska, 1994; Watters, Estilo, Clark, & Lorvick, 1994). However, even when sterile needles are available and inexpensive, factors including apathy, social custom, a sense of urgency, and psychological distress may reduce their perceived availability or affordability (Black et al., 1986; Strathdee et al., 1997). Other factors that may be related to sharing needles include severity of drug use, psychopathology, and gender. The former variable, severity of use, has been found to be significantly correlated with the risk of sharing. Specifically, injection drug users (IDUs) who inject more frequently and who inject drug combinations are significantly more likely to use borrowed needles (Klee, Faugier, Hayes, Boulton, & Morris, 1990; Watters et al., 1994).

Level of psychopathology has been explored, and studies have revealed a consistently positive relationship between needle sharing and psychiatric symptoms, especially depression (Hawkins, Latkin, Chowdury, & Hawkins, 1998; Mandell, Kim, Latkin, & Suh, 1999; Strathdee et al., 1997). Various hypotheses have attempted to explain this relationship, including the possibilities that individuals with depressive symptoms may receive needed social interaction and support from their drug network (Latkin & Mandell, 1993; Suh, Mandell, & Kim, 1997), that depression may predispose individuals toward feelings of lack of control or power (Green & Kreuter, 1991), and that depressed individuals may engage in risky health behaviors because they do not anticipate a positive future.

The relationship between sharing and gender has also received attention, with findings pointing toward an increased likelihood of sharing behavior among female IDUs (Darke, Ross, Cohen, Hando, & Hall, 1995; Wang, Siegal, Falck, & Carlson, 1998). Some of the same dynamics present among depressed individuals that may result in sharing behaviors may also be present among women. For example, Soet, Dudley, and Dilorio (1999) found that low perceived power among women affected their sexual decision making, resulting in more risk behaviors. Although research has provided evidence that women tend to endorse higher levels of psychopathology than men (Johnson, Brems, & Fisher, 1996; McGrath, Strickland, Keita, & Russo,

---

[16] Johnson, M. E., Yep, M. J., Brems, C., Theno, S. A., & Fisher, D. G. (2002). Relationship among gender, depression, and needle sharing in a sample of injection drug users. *Psychology of Addictive Behaviors, 16*, 338–341.

1990; Rabkin et al., 1997), including higher levels of depression (Brienza et al., 2000), no study has yet explored whether gender and depression interact in their relationship with needle sharing.

Using a sample of street drug users, in the current study we examined the relationships among gender, depression, and needle sharing. We hypothesized that needle sharers would report higher levels of depression than nonsharers, that women would report higher levels of depression than men, and that female sharers would report the highest levels of depression among all other groups.

___ 1. Does the researcher begin by identifying a specific problem area?

Very satisfactory   5 (4) 3 2 1   Very unsatisfactory   *or*   N/A   I/I

___ 2. Does the researcher establish the importance of the problem area?

Very satisfactory   5 4 3 2 1   Very unsatisfactory   *or*   N/A (I/I)

___ 3. Are any underlying theories adequately described?

Very satisfactory   5 4 3 2 (1) Very unsatisfactory   *or*   N/A   I/I

___ 4. Does the introduction move from topic to topic instead of from citation to citation?

Very satisfactory   5 4 3 2 1   Very unsatisfactory   *or* (N/A) I/I

___ 5. Is the research a coherent essay with logical transitions from topic to topic?

Very satisfactory   5 4 3 2 1   Very unsatisfactory   *or* (N/A) I/I

___ 6. Has the researcher provided conceptual definitions of key terms?

Very satisfactory   5 4 3 2 1   Very unsatisfactory   *or* (N/A) I/I

___ 7. Has the researcher indicated the basis for "factual" statements?

Very satisfactory   5 4 3 (2) 1   Very unsatisfactory   *or*   N/A   I/I

___ 8. Do the specific research purposes, questions, or hypotheses logically flow from the introductory material?

Very satisfactory   5 4 3 2 1   Very unsatisfactory   *or* (N/A) I/I

___ 9. Overall, is the introduction effective and appropriate?

Very satisfactory   5 4 3 2 (1) Very unsatisfactory   *or*   N/A   I/I

Part B

Directions: Read several research reports in academic journals on a topic of interest to you. Apply the evaluation questions in this chapter to the introductions, and select the one to which you have given the highest ratings. Bring it to class for discussion. Be prepared to discuss its strengths and weaknesses.

Chapter 5

A Closer Look at Evaluating Literature Reviews

As you learned in the previous chapter, literature reviews usually are integrated into the researcher's introductory statements. In that chapter, the emphasis was on the functions of the introduction and the most salient and easy-to-evaluate characteristics of a literature review. In this chapter, we will examine evaluation questions regarding the presentation of the literature that are important but sometimes difficult to evaluate.

___ **1. If there is extensive literature on a topic, has the researcher been selective?**

Very satisfactory 5 4 3 2 1 Very unsatisfactory *or* N/A I/I

Comment: Of course, you may not know if the research on a topic is extensive unless you have studied the topic in detail or unless the researcher describes its breadth. Even in the absence of this information, you can still spot certain flaws related to this evaluation question. First, look for long strings of references used to support a single point or position. This is often a sign that the researcher has not been selective in choosing research to cite.[1] Example 5.1.1 illustrates this flaw. Example 5.1.2 shows an improved version. Notice that "e.g." (meaning "for example") is appropriately used in Example 5.1.2.

Example 5.1.1[2]
Unselective referencing (inappropriate):

Several issues must be addressed before grade-sensitive indices can be identified. The first is how to identify expert literacy teachers. In the past, some researchers have asked teachers to identify their own competencies (Dillman, 1978; Warwick & Lininger, 1975; Hoover & Johnson, 1998; James, 2001; Kelp, 2002; Koontz, Doe, & Jones, 2002; Kibler & Loone, 2003; Stansky & Lip, 2003; First, Hadley, & Palms, 2003; Doe, 2003).

---

[1] Long strings of references for a single point are more justifiable in a thesis or dissertation, especially if the committee that is evaluating it expects a student to produce a comprehensive review to demonstrate that he or she can locate all the literature related to a topic.

[2] This example was modified from the original to illustrate an *inappropriate* technique. The original and its reference is given in Example 5.1.2.

Example 5.1.2[3]

Selective referencing (citing only important references):

Several issues must be addressed before grade-sensitive indices can be identified. The first is how to identify expert literacy teachers. In the past, some researchers have asked teachers to assess their own competencies (e.g., Dillman, 1978; Warwick & Lininger, 1975).

___ **2. Is the literature review critical?**

Very satisfactory 5 4 3 2 1 Very unsatisfactory *or* N/A I/I

Comment: A researcher should consider the strengths and weaknesses of previously published studies. Articles that are reasonably strong may be cited without comment on their methodological merits. Also, a researcher may feel it unnecessary to point out weaknesses in previously published research reports when their results have been corroborated (or replicated) by other, more methodologically sound research that is also cited in the review. However, when the results of several studies contradict one another, researchers usually should point out which ones may be more dependable than the others or note that all are weak when that is the case. Example 5.2.1, which is taken from the introduction to a study on the development of eating disorders, illustrates this technique.

Example 5.2.1[4]

Critical excerpt from a literature review:

However, our review of the literature indicates that, to date, only one prospective longitudinal study has systematically investigated the association between several different types of psychiatric disorders and the subsequent development of eating disorders during adolescence. Zaider et al. (in press) reported findings suggesting that depressive disorders may play a particularly important role in the development of eating disorders during adolescence. However, the sample studied by Zaider et al. was modest in size, and Axis I psychiatric disorders were assessed with a self-report questionnaire. Further research, involving the administration of structured diagnostic interviews to a larger and more representative sample, is needed to investigate more extensively the association between a wide range of psychiatric disorders during early

---

[3] Block, C. C., Oakar, M., & Hurt, N. (2002). The expertise of literacy teachers: A continuum from preschool to Grade 5. *Reading Research Quarterly, 37*, 178–206.

[4] Johnson, J. G., Cohen, P., Kotler, L., Kasen, S., & Brook, J. S. (2002). Psychiatric disorders associated with risk for the development of eating disorders during adolescence and early adulthood. *Journal of Consulting and Clinical Psychology, 70*, 1119–1128.

adolescence and the subsequent development of eating disorders. It is of particular interest to investigate this association during adolescence and early adulthood because eating disorders and many other types of psychiatric disorders tend to first become evident during these developmental periods.

Sometimes criticism is subtle, as in Example 5.2.2, where the researchers have hedged their generalizations from the literature as indicated by the italicized words. Notice how these words suggest that caution should be used when considering the results. If you read the example a second time, leaving out the italicized words, you will get a very different impression of the state of knowledge on this topic.

Example 5.2.2[5]

Excerpt from a literature review (subtle criticism expressing caution, italics added):

However, though less attention has been given to personality factors, there is *some* evidence that affective-based or dispositional correlates are related to emotional exhaustion (Cordes & Dougherty, 1993). Consequently, *it might be that* affective personality dispositions are accounting for the relationship between emotional exhaustion and various work outcomes. Lee and Ashforth (1996) noted the need for research *providing additional clarification* of these *proposed* relationships.

Of course, a researcher might also want to point out strengths of particular studies along the way—especially if they are promising studies on which the current one is closely based.

___ 3. Is current research cited?

Very satisfactory 5 4 3 2 1 Very unsatisfactory *or* N/A I/I

Comment: You can check the currency of the literature by noting whether research published in recent years has been cited. Keep in mind, however, that relevance to the research topic is more important than currency. A ten-year-old study that is highly relevant may deserve more attention than a less relevant one that was recently published.

Also note that a researcher may want to establish the historical context for his or her study. A historical context might help establish the legitimacy of the current studies a researcher is presenting. In Example 5.3.1, the researcher links

---

[5] Wright, T. A., & Cropanzano, R. (1998). Emotional exhaustion as a predictor of job performance and voluntary turnover. *Journal of Applied Psychology, 83*, 486–493.

a particular finding back to Piaget, an important and widely cited researcher in child development. This historical linkage adds support to the point being made by suggesting that the finding has stood the test of time by being replicated more recently.

Example 5.3.1[6]

An excerpt from a literature review showing historical links:

According to research carried out by Piaget (1932) and subsequently by Wimmer, Gruber, and Perner (1984) and Strichartz and Burton (1990), young children have little or no understanding of lying as deceptive statements intended to mislead others. They regard all falsehoods as lies and do not recognize that a genuine mistake by a speaker who believes that he or she has made a true statement is not a lie.

___ 4. Has the researcher distinguished between opinions and research findings?

Very satisfactory 5 4 3 2 1 Very unsatisfactory *or* N/A I/I

Comment: Researchers should use wording that helps readers understand whether the cited literature presents opinions or research results.

For indicating that a citation is research based, there are a variety of options, a number of which are shown in Example 5.4.1.

Example 5.4.1

Examples of key terms and expressions indicating that a citation is research based:

Recent data suggest that....

In laboratory experiments....

Recent test scores suggest....

Group A has outperformed its counterparts on measures of....

Research on XYZ has....

Data from surveys comparing....

Doe (1999) found that the rate....

These studies have greatly increased our knowledge of....

---

[6] Siegal, M. (1998). Preschoolers' understanding of lies and innocent and negligent mistakes. *Developmental Psychology, 2*, 332–341.

In addition, if a researcher cites a specific statistic from the literature (e.g., "In Australia, from 1991 to 2000 there was a 54% increase in higher degree research enrollments [Kemp, 2001]"[7]), it is safe to assume that research is being cited.

Sometimes researchers cite the opinions of others. When they do this, they should word their statements in such a way that readers are made aware that opinions (and not research findings) are being cited. Example 5.4.2 shows some examples of key words and phrases that researchers sometimes use to do this.

Example 5.4.2
Examples of key terms and expressions indicating that an opinion is being cited:

Jones (1999) has argued that….

These kinds of assumptions were….

Despite this speculation….

These arguments predict….

This logical suggestion….

Smith has strongly advocated the use of….

___ **5. Has the researcher distinguished between what is proposed by a theory and research findings related to the theory?**

Very satisfactory 5 4 3 2 1 Very unsatisfactory *or* N/A I/I

Comment: When citing a premise from theory, a researcher should simply use the word "theory" and distinguish it from research findings related to the theory. Example 5.5.1 shows two consecutive paragraphs. The first clearly is a description of attachment theory while the second one describes research results related to the theory.

Example 5.5.1[8]
Excerpt indicating the distinction between theory and research results (italics added for emphasis):

According to attachment theory, the relation between quality of early care and infant security holds across a wide range of cultures and contexts. To be clear, Bowlby (1982) proposed the attachment behavioral system to be

---

[7] Smith, L. (2002). Quality postgraduate research programs and student experience. *The Australian Electronic Journal of Nursing Education, 8,* accessed at http://www.scu.edu.au/schools/nhcp/aejne/vol8-1/refereed/smith_post.html on January 3, 2003.
[8] Posada, G. et al. (2002). Maternal caregiving and infant security in two cultures. *Developmental Psychology, 38,* 67–78.

a species-characteristic product common to all children reared within the range of our environment of evolutionary adaptedness. This can be understood as a propensity to organize an attachment behavioral system and develop an attachment relationship within the context of child–caregiver interactions (Posada et al., 1995). Further, Bowlby (1982) and Ainsworth et al. (1978) proposed that the specific quality of an attachment relationship depends on the particular history of child–caregiver interactions.

Research findings indicate that the secure-base phenomenon is common to children from different cultures and socioeconomic contexts (e.g., Ainsworth, 1967; Anderson, 1972; Posada et al., 1995). They also show that rates of secure attachment in children are lower in families under stress than in families under low-stress (usually middle-class) conditions (Posada et al., 1995; Posada et al., 1999; Valenzuela, 1990; Vaughn, Egeland, Sroufe, & Waters, 1979) and vary from culture to culture (Grossmann, Grossmann, Spangler, Suess, & Unzner, 1985; Mikaye, Chen, & Campos, 1985; Takahashi, 1986; van Ijzendoorn & Kroonenberg, 1988). These latter results regarding rates of secure and insecure attachments are not inconsistent with *attachment theory*.

___ **6. Overall, is the literature review portion of the introduction appropriate?**

Very satisfactory   5   4   3   2   1   Very unsatisfactory   *or*   N/A   I/I

Comment: Rate this evaluation question after considering your answers to the earlier ones in this chapter and any additional considerations and concerns you may have. Be prepared to explain your overall evaluation.

Exercise for Chapter 5

Part A

Directions: Answer the following questions.

1. Do you agree that a long string of references to support a single point is usually inappropriate? (See Evaluation Question 1.) Instead, would you support the argument that citing a large number of references shows that there is great support for the point being made? Does a large number indicate that the researcher has conducted a thorough literature review?

2. Consider Statement A and Statement B below. They both contain the same citations. In your opinion, which statement is superior? Explain.

> Statement A: "The overall positive association between nonverbal decoding skills and workplace effectiveness has replicated with adults in a variety of settings (Campbell, Kagan, & Krathwohl, 1971; Costanzo & Philpott, 1986; Schag, Loo, & Levin, 1978; DiMatteo, Friedman, & Taranta, 1979; Tickle-Degnen, 1998; Halberstadt & Hall, 1980; Izard, 1971; Izard et al., 2001; Nowicki & Duke, 1994)."

> Statement B: "The overall positive association between nonverbal decoding skills and workplace effectiveness has replicated with adults in counseling settings (Campbell, Kagan, & Krathwohl, 1971; Costanzo & Philpott, 1986; Schag, Loo, & Levin, 1978) and medical settings (DiMatteo, Friedman, & Taranta, 1979; Tickle-Degnen, 1998) and with children in academic settings (Halberstadt & Hall, 1980; Izard, 1971; Izard et al., 2001; Nowicki & Duke, 1994)."[9]

3. Consider Statement C and Statement D below. Does the term "well established in the literature" in Statement D influence your interpretation of the statement? Explain.

> Statement C: "Parents and grandparents provide protective influence on pregnant and parenting adolescents' well-being (Apfel & Seitz, 1996; Wilson, 1986). However, far less attention has been paid to the role of siblings."

> Statement D: "Although the protective influence of parent and grandparent support on pregnant and parenting adolescents' well-being has been well established in the literature (Apfel & Seitz, 1996; Wilson, 1986), far less attention has been paid to the role of siblings."[10]

4. Consider a topic of special interest to you in your professional field. In your opinion, would it be important for a research report on that topic to contain a historical background (i.e., context)? Explain.

Part B

Directions: Read several research reports in academic journals on a topic of interest to you. Apply the evaluation questions in this chapter to the literature reviews in their introductions, and select the one to which you gave the highest

---

[9] Effenbein, H. A., & Ambady, N. (2002). Predicting workplace outcomes from the ability to eavesdrop on feelings. *Journal of Applied Psychology, 87, 963–971.*

[10] Gee, C. B., Nicholson, M. J., Osborne, L. N., & Rhodes, J. E. (2003). Support and strain in pregnant and parenting adolescents' sibling relationships. *Journal of Adolescent Research, 18, 25–35.*

ratings. Bring it to class for discussion. Be prepared to discuss its specific strengths and weaknesses. Also, examine it to see if it has at least one example of each of the following. If so, mark the examples and be prepared to discuss them in class.

5. A positive, critical statement about literature being cited (e.g., In a well-designed study, Smith (2003) found....).

6. A negative, critical statement about literature being cited (e.g., Because of the high attrition rate, it is difficult to interpret Smith's findings.).

7. An opinion expressed by the researcher that is explicitly introduced as such with terms such as "speculation" and "logical argument."

8. A statement about a theory (clearly identified as theory) with a research finding (clearly identified as a research finding) relating to the theory.

Chapter 6

Evaluating Samples When Researchers Generalize

Immediately after the introduction, which includes a literature review, most researchers insert a main heading titled "Method." In the method section, researchers almost always begin by describing the people they studied—their sample. This description is usually prefaced with one of these subheadings: "Participants"[1] or "Subjects."

A *population* is any group in which a researcher is ultimately interested. It may be large, such as all registered voters in Pennsylvania, or it may be small, such as all members of a local teachers' association. Researchers often study only a *sample* (i.e., a subset of a population) for the sake of efficiency and then *generalize* their results to the population, that is, they infer that the data they collected by studying the sample are similar to the data they would have obtained by studying the entire population.

Because many researchers do not explicitly state whether they are attempting to generalize, you will often need to make a judgment on this matter in order to decide whether to apply the evaluation questions in this chapter to each research report you are evaluating. Does the researcher *imply* that the results apply to some larger population? Does the researcher discuss the implications of his or her research for a larger group than the one directly studied? Note that the answers to these questions may be found anywhere in a research report, so you will need to read the entire report before answering them. If the answers are clearly "yes," you should apply the evaluation questions in this chapter to the article you have read. Note that the evaluation of samples when researchers are *not* attempting to generalize to a population is considered in Chapter 7.

___ 1. Was random sampling used?

Very satisfactory 5 4 3 2 1 Very unsatisfactory *or* N/A I/I

Comment: Using random sampling (like drawing names out of a hat) yields an *unbiased* sample (i.e., a sample that does not systematically favor any particular

---

[1] For most of the 1900s, the standard subheading was "Subjects." Near the end of the century, "Participants" became popular. The latter term indicates that the people being studied have consented to participate after being informed of the nature of the research project, its potential benefits, and its potential harm.

type of individual or group in the selection process). If a sample is unbiased and large, researchers are likely to make sound generalizations. (Sample size will be discussed later in this chapter.)

The desirability of using random samples as the basis for making generalizations is so widely recognized among researchers that they are almost certain to mention its use if they have used it. This is illustrated in Example 6.1.1, in which a random sample of 50% of a population was selected.

Example 6.1.1[2]
Brief description of the use of random sampling:

The owner of Beyond Hearing [an Internet-based support group for individuals with hearing loss] made available the entire list of members, allowing us to draw a random sample, and posted a message to members informing them of this project and endorsing its research goals. We sent a 34-item e-mail survey to a random sample of 50% of Beyond Hearing members....

___ 2. If random sampling was used, was it stratified?

Very satisfactory 5 4 3 2 1 Very unsatisfactory *or* N/A I/I

Comment: Researchers use *stratified random sampling* by drawing individuals separately at random from different strata (i.e., subgroups) within a population. Suppose a researcher wants to survey licensed clinical psychologists in a large city. To stratify, he or she might divide the population into four subgroups: those who practice on the north side of town, those who practice on the east side, and so on. Then he or she could draw a fixed percentage at random from each side of town. The result will be a sample that is geographically representative. For instance, if 40% of the population practices on the west side, then 40% of the sample will be from the west side.

Stratifying will improve a sample only if the stratification variable ("geography" in our example) is related to the variables to be studied. For instance, if the researcher is planning to study how psychologists work with illicit substance abusers, stratifying on geography will improve the sample if the various areas of the city tend to have different types of drug problems, which may require different treatment modalities.

Note that *geography* is often an excellent variable on which to stratify because people tend to cluster geographically based on many variables that are important in the social and behavioral sciences. For example, they often cluster according to race/ethnicity, income/personal wealth, language preference,

---

[2] Cummings, J. N., Sproull, L., & Kiesler, S. B. (2002). Beyond hearing: Where real-world and online support meet. *Group Dynamics: Theory, Research, & Practice, 6*, 78–88.

religion, and so on. Thus, a geographically representative sample is likely to be representative in terms of these other variables as well.

Other common stratification variables are occupation, highest educational level attained, political affiliation, and age, which was used in Example 6.2.1. Notice that the strata are referred to as cohorts in this example.

Example 6.2.1[3]

Description of the use of stratified random sampling:

The sample was stratified by age and gender into three 5-year cohorts: 70–74, 75–79, 80–84, and a fourth cohort of individuals over 85 years of age. Randomly sampled individuals from within these cohorts were invited to participate in the [study] on a voluntary basis.

If random sampling without stratification is used, the technique is called *simple random sampling*. On the other hand, if stratification is used to form subgroups from which random samples are drawn, the technique is called *stratified random sampling*.

Despite the almost universal acceptance that an unbiased sample obtained through simple or stratified random sampling is highly desirable for making generalizations, the vast majority of research from which researchers want to make generalizations is based on studies in which nonrandom (biased) samples were used. There are three major reasons for this:

1. Even though a random selection of names has been drawn, the researcher may not be able to convince all those selected to participate in the research project. For example, the researchers who wrote the material in Example 6.2.1 had only a 55% response rate (i.e., only 55% of the individuals they contacted agreed to participate). It is important to note that those who did respond may be systematically different from those who did not in many important ways (e.g., because they were less interested in the topic, did not wish to talk with strangers, or were not physically able to participate). Thus, the bias created by the failure of many to participate could seriously affect the results of a study.

2. Many researchers have limited resources: limited time, money, and assistance to conduct research. Often, they will reach out for individuals who are readily accessible or convenient to use as participants. For instance, college professors conducting research often find that the most convenient samples consist of students enrolled in their classes, which are not even random samples of students on a campus.

3. For some populations, it is difficult to identify all members. If a researcher cannot do this, he or she obviously cannot give each of them an equal

---

[3] Anstey, K. J., Luszcz, M. A., Giles, L. C., & Andrews, G. R. (2001). Demographic, health, cognitive, and sensory variables as predictors of mortality in very old adults. *Psychology and Aging, 16*, 3–11.

chance of having their names drawn. Examples of populations of this type are the homeless in a large city and successful burglars (i.e., those who have never been caught).

Because so many researchers study nonrandom samples, it is unrealistic to count failures on the first two evaluation questions in this chapter as fatal flaws in research methodology. If journal editors routinely refused to publish research reports with this type of deficiency, there would be very little, if any, published research on most of the important problems in the social and behavioral sciences. Thus, when researchers use nonrandom samples when attempting to generalize, the additional evaluation questions raised below should be applied in order to distinguish between studies from which it might be reasonable to make tentative, cautious generalizations and those that are hopelessly flawed in this respect.

___ **3. If the randomness of a sample is impaired by the refusal to participate by some of those selected, is the rate of participation reasonably high?**

Very satisfactory 5 4 3 2 1 Very unsatisfactory *or* N/A I/I

Comment: Defining "reasonably high" is problematic. For example, a professional survey organization, with trained personnel and substantial resources, would be concerned if it had a response rate of less than 85% when conducting a national survey by phone or in person. On the other hand, researchers with limited resources using mailed questionnaires often are satisfied with a return rate as low as 60%, especially because rates of returns to mailed surveys are often notoriously poor. As a very rough rule-of-thumb, then, response rates of substantially less than 60% raise very serious concerns about the generalizability of the findings.

The percentages mentioned in the previous paragraph should not be applied mechanically when evaluating research because you might make exceptions for instances in which participation in the research is burdensome, invasive, or raises sensitive issues—factors that might make it difficult to get a high rate of participation. For instance, if a researcher needed to draw samples of blood from students on campus to estimate the incidence of HIV infection or needed to put a sample of students through a series of physical fitness tests that spanned several days for a study in sports psychology, you might judge a participation rate of substantially less than 60% to be reasonable in light of the particulars of the research, keeping in mind that any generalizations would be highly tenuous.

When applying this evaluation question, you may also want to consider how much effort a researcher put into trying to obtain a high rate of participation. For example, if a researcher contacted those who were selected several times (by phone, by mail, or in person) and still had a response rate of less than 60%, you might reach the conclusion that this is the highest rate of return that might be expected for the researcher's particular research problem and population. In effect, you might judge that this is the best that can be done, keeping in mind that generalizations from such a sample are exceedingly risky because nonparticipants might be fundamentally different from those who participated. Example 6.3.1 describes the extensive efforts made to obtain a sample of married couples in the general (not college) population. Note that despite their efforts, the response rate was only 37%.

Example 6.3.1[4]

Extensive efforts to obtain a sample:

A mailing list with a random sample of married persons in a large metropolitan area was obtained from a commercial mail-distribution source. A four-step mailing procedure was used to maximize the response rate (Sheskin, 1985). The first step involved sending a postcard to 350 married individuals (175 couples) informing them that they would receive a request for participation and a packet of questionnaires in the next week. There were 18 (10%) postcards that were not deliverable. The questionnaires were sent with instructions for each spouse to complete the questionnaires privately and return them separately to the researcher in the envelopes provided. A financial incentive of $20 was offered to couples who completed the questionnaires. Potential respondents who did not complete the questionnaires 2 weeks after they were mailed were sent a reminder postcard. If the questionnaires were not received within 4 weeks after they were mailed, a second set of materials was sent. Following this procedure, 116 (37%) questionnaires were returned, 6 of which were not usable.

___ **4. If the randomness of a sample is impaired by the refusal to participate by some of those selected, is there reason to believe that the participants and nonparticipants are similar on relevant variables?**

Very satisfactory   5   4   3   2   1   Very unsatisfactory   *or*   N/A   I/I

Comment: Sometimes researchers have information about those who do not participate, which allows for a comparison of the two groups. For example, a researcher might note the zip codes in which returned questionnaires were

---

[4] Fowers, B. J., Lyons, E., Montel, K. H., & Shaked, N. (2001). Positive illusions about marriage among married and single individuals. *Journal of Family Psychology, 15*, 95–109.

posted. This might allow a researcher to determine whether those in affluent neighborhoods were more responsive than those in less affluent ones.[5]

In institutional settings such as schools, hospitals, and prisons, it is often possible to determine whether participants and nonparticipants differ in important respects. For instance, in a survey regarding political attitudes held by college students, participants might be asked for background information such as major, GPA, and age. These background characteristics are probably known for all students on the campus, allowing for a comparison of participants and the whole student body. If there are substantial differences, the results will need to be interpreted in light of them. For instance, if political science majors formed a larger percentage of the participants than exists in the whole student body, the researcher should be highly cautious in interpreting the resulting data.

In the evaluation of a new component for the Head Start program in rural areas of Oregon, only 56% agreed to participate. The researchers noted, however, the similarities of these participants with the general population in Example 6.4.1. This gives us some assurance that those who chose to participate were not extremely different from nonparticipants in terms of important background characteristics (i.e., demographics).

Example 6.4.1[6]
Comparison of a flawed sample with a larger group:

...45% of children [were] living in families including both biological parents. Sixty percent of the children and families received public assistance. Eighty-three percent were Caucasian, and 13% were other ethnic groups, primarily Hispanic. These demographics are representative of the rural population in Oregon.

___ **5. If a sample from which a researcher wants to generalize was not selected at random, is it at least drawn from the target group for the generalization?**

Very satisfactory 5 4 3 2 1 Very unsatisfactory *or* N/A I/I

Comment: There are many instances in the published literature in which a researcher studied one type of participant (e.g., college freshmen) and used the data to make generalizations to an entirely different target group (e.g., public school students). If a researcher does not have the wherewithal to at least tap into the target group of interest, it might be better if he or she left the research

---

[5] If such a bias were detected, statistical adjustments might be made to correct for it by mathematically giving more weight to the respondents from the underrepresented zip codes.
[6] Kaminski, R. A., Stormshak, E. A., Good, R. H. III, & Goodman, M. R. (2002). Prevention of substance abuse with rural Head Start children and families: Results of Project STAR. *Psychology of Addictive Behaviors, 16*, S11–S26.

to others with resources and contacts that give them access to members of the target group.

There are also many instances in which the nonrandom sample is drawn from a *specialized subgroup* from the population to which the researcher wants to generalize. For example, in a campus survey of athletes' attitudes toward performance-enhancing drugs, members of only certain athletic teams may be available, calling into question the generalizability of the results to all athletes on the campus.

___ 6. If a sample from which a researcher wants to generalize was not selected at random, is it at least reasonably diverse?

Very satisfactory 5 4 3 2 1 Very unsatisfactory *or* N/A I/I

Comment: Did a researcher generalize to all college students after studying only students attending a small religious college in which 99% of the students have the same ethnic/racial background? Did a researcher generalize to men and women regarding the relationship between exercise and health after studying only men attending a cardiac unit's exercise program? An answer of "yes" to these questions might cause you to give a low rating to this evaluation question.

___ 7. If a sample from which a researcher wants to generalize was not selected at random, does the researcher explicitly discuss this limitation?

Very satisfactory 5 4 3 2 1 Very unsatisfactory *or* N/A I/I

Comment: While researchers may discuss the limitations of their methodology (including sampling) in any part of their reports, many include a discussion of the limitations in the discussion/conclusion section at the end. In Example 6.7.1, the researchers discuss their low rate of response as a limitation and discuss some of the difficulties associated with getting a low rate of response in Internet surveys. Since they were studying victimization and on-line dating, they note in the second paragraph that some of the most important participants for their study may have stopped using the Internet, making it impossible to survey them via the Internet.

Example 6.7.1[7]
Statement of a limitation in sampling:

This study also is limited in its sample response rate. We recognize that

[7] Jerin, R., Dolinsky, B., & College, E. (2001). You've got mail! You don't want it: Cyber-victimization and on-line dating. *Journal of Criminal Justice and Popular Culture, 9*, 15–21.

the low response rate can impact external validity, and this has been acknowledged by researchers using on-line surveying (Cho & LaRose, 1999). While our response may initially seem very low, it may not be. Sampling on the Web and using e-mail to contact subjects make it impossible to distinguish between those who actually received and declined to respond to a survey and those who never received the survey at all (Kaye & Johnson, 1999).

It would also be reasonable to assume that most women who have been victimized over the Internet may have stopped using it. Identifying those women who have been victimized and gathering data on their experiences is imperative. We also acknowledge that there is a need for information on individuals' experiences with on-line dating and how it compares to traditional methods of meeting romantic partners. There has been very limited research systematically examining the nature of cyber-relationships (Fagan, 2001; Griffiths, 2000).

Such acknowledgments of limitations do not improve researchers' ability to generalize. However, they do perform two important functions: (a) they serve as warnings to naïve readers regarding the problem of generalizing and (b) they reassure all readers that the researchers are aware of a serious flaw in their methodology—a sign of the researchers' overall competence.

____ 8. Has the author described relevant demographics of the sample?

Very satisfactory 5 4 3 2 1 Very unsatisfactory *or* N/A I/I

Comment: A researcher should describe the relevant demographics (i.e., background characteristics). For example, when studying registered nurses' attitudes toward assisted suicide, it would be relevant to know their religious affiliations. For studying consumers' preferences, it would be helpful to know their economic status.

In addition to demographics that are directly relevant to the variables being studied, it usually is desirable to give an overall demographic profile, including variables such as age, gender, race/ethnicity, and highest level of education. This is especially important when a sample of convenience has been used because readers will want to visualize the particular participants who were part of such a sample.

____ 9. Is the overall size of the sample adequate?

Very satisfactory 5 4 3 2 1 Very unsatisfactory *or* N/A I/I

Comment: Students who are new to research methods are sometimes surprised to learn that there often is no simple answer to the question of how large a sample should be. First, it depends in part on how much error a researcher is willing to tolerate. For public opinion polls, a sample size of 1,500 drawn at random produces a margin of error of about one to three percentage points. A sample size of 400 produces a margin of error of about four to six percentage points.[8] If a researcher is trying to predict the outcome of a close election, clearly a sample size of 400 would be inadequate.[9]

Responding to a public opinion poll takes little time and may be of interest to many participants. Other types of studies, however, may require extensive cooperation and effort on the part of participants as well as the expenditure of considerable resources by the researchers. Under such circumstances, it may be unrealistic to expect a researcher to use hundreds of participants. Thus, you should ask whether the researchers used a reasonable number given the particular circumstances of their studies. Would it have been an unreasonable burden to use substantially more participants? Is the number of participants so low that there is little hope of making sound generalizations? Would you base an important decision on the results of the study given the number of participants used? Your subjective answers to these types of questions will guide you on this evaluation question.[10]

It is important to keep in mind that a large sample size does not compensate for a bias in sampling due to the failure to use random sampling, that is, using large numbers of unrepresentative participants does not get around the problem of their unrepresentativeness.

___10. Is the number of participants in each group sufficiently large?

Very satisfactory 5 4 3 2 1 Very unsatisfactory *or* N/A I/I

Comment: Consider the hypothetical information in Example 6.10.1, where the numbers of participants in each subgroup are indicated by *n*, and the mean (average) scores are indicated by *m*.

Example 6.10.1
A sample in which some subgroups are very small:

A random sample of 100 college freshmen was surveyed on its knowledge

---

[8] The exact size of the margin of error depends on whether the sample was stratified and other sampling issues that are beyond the scope of this book.

[9] With a sample of only 400 individuals, there would need to be an 8 to 12 percentage-point *difference* (twice the four- to six-point margin of error) between the two candidates to make a reliable prediction (i.e., statistically significant prediction).

[10] There are statistical methods for estimating optimum sample sizes under various assumptions. While these methods are beyond the scope of this book, note that they do not take into account the practical matters raised here.

of alcoholism. The mean (m) scores out of a maximum of 25 were as follows: White ($m = 18.5$, $n = 78$), African American ($m = 20.1$, $n = 11$), Hispanic/Latino(a) ($m = 19.9$, $n = 9$), and Chinese American ($m = 17.9$, $n = 2$). Thus, for each of the four ethnic/racial groups, there was a reasonably high average knowledge of alcoholism.

Although the total number in the sample is 100 (a number that would be considered rather low for most research purposes), the numbers of participants in the last three subgroups in the example are so small that it would be highly inappropriate to generalize from them to their respective populations. The researcher should either obtain larger numbers of them or refrain from separately reporting on them. Notice that there is nothing wrong with indicating ethnic/racial backgrounds (such as the fact that there were two Chinese American participants) as part of the description of the demographics of the sample. Instead, the problem is that the number of them is too small to justify calculating a mean and making an inference about a population of Chinese Americans. In other words, a mean of 17.9 for the two Chinese Americans is meaningless for a survey of this type.

___11. Has informed consent been obtained?

Very satisfactory 5 4 3 2 1 Very unsatisfactory *or* N/A I/I

Comment: It is almost always a good idea to get written, informed consent from the participants in a study. Participants should be informed of the nature of the study and, at least in general terms, the nature of their involvement. They should also be informed of their right to withdraw from the study at any time without penalty. Typically, researchers report only very briefly on this matter, as illustrated in Example 6.11.1, which presents a statement similar to many found in research reports in academic journals. It is unrealistic to expect much more detail than shown here because, by convention, the discussion of this issue is typically brief. Note that this evaluation question also appears in the next chapter for reasons that you will learn when you read it.

Example 6.11.1
Brief description of informed consent:

Students from the departmental subject pool volunteered to participate in this study for course credit. Prior to participating in the study, students were given an informed consent form that had been approved by the university's institutional review board. The form described the experiment as "a study of social interactions between male and female students" and informed them that if they consented, they were free to withdraw from the study at any time without penalty.

There will be times when you judge that the study is so innocuous that informed consent might not be needed. A good example is an observational study in which people are observed in public places, such as a public park or shopping mall, while the observers are in plain view. Under such circumstances, privacy would not normally be expected.

___ 12. Overall, is the sample appropriate for generalizing?

Very satisfactory 5 4 3 2 1 Very unsatisfactory *or* N/A I/I

Comment: Rate this evaluation question after considering your answers to the earlier ones in this chapter and any additional considerations and concerns you may have. Be prepared to discuss your response to this evaluation question.

Concluding Comment

Although a primary goal of much research in all the sciences is to make sound generalizations from samples to populations, researchers in the social and behavioral sciences face special problems regarding access to and cooperation from samples of humans. Unlike other published lists of criteria for evaluating samples, I have urged you to be pragmatic when making these evaluations. A researcher may have some relatively serious flaws in sampling, yet you may conclude that he or she did a reasonable job under the circumstances he or she faced. However, this does not preclude the need to be exceedingly cautious in making generalizations from studies with weak samples. Our confidence in certain generalizations based on weak samples can be increased, however, if various researchers with different patterns of weaknesses in their sampling methods arrive at similar conclusions when studying the same problems.

In the next chapter, we will consider the evaluation of samples when researchers do *not* attempt to generalize.

Exercise for Chapter 6

Part A

Directions: Answer the following questions.

1. Suppose a researcher conducted a survey on a college campus by interviewing students that she/he approached while they were having dinner in the campus cafeteria one evening. In your opinion, is this a "random sample" of all students enrolled in the college? Even if you think it is not random, is it a reasonably good way to sample? Explain.

2. Briefly explain why *geography* is often an excellent variable on which to stratify when sampling.

3. According to this chapter, the vast majority of research is based on biased samples. Cite one reason that is given in this chapter for this circumstance.

4. If extensive efforts have been made to increase the rate of participation, and yet the response rate is low, how would you be willing to give the report a reasonably high rating for sampling? Explain.

5. Is it important to know whether participants and nonparticipants are similar on relevant variables? Explain.

6. Does the use of a large sample compensate for a bias in sampling? Explain.

Part B

Directions: Locate several research reports in academic journals in which the researchers are concerned with generalizing from a sample to a population and apply the evaluation questions in this chapter. Select the one to which you gave the highest overall rating and bring it to class for discussion. Be prepared to discuss the strengths and weaknesses of the sampling method used.

Chapter 7

Evaluating Samples When Researchers Do *Not* Generalize

As you know from the previous chapter, researchers often study samples in order to make inferences about the populations from which the samples were drawn. This process is known as generalizing.

Not all research is aimed at generalizing. Here are the major reasons why:

1. Researchers often conduct *pilot studies*. These are designed to determine the feasibility of methods for studying specific research problems. For example, a novice researcher who wants to conduct an interview study of the social dynamics of safe-sex practices among high school students might conduct a pilot study to determine, among other things, how much cooperation can be obtained from school personnel for such a study, what percentage of the parents give permission for their children to participate in interviews on this topic, whether students have difficulty understanding the interview questions and whether they are embarrassed by them, the optimum length of the interviews, and so on. After the research techniques are refined in a pilot study with a sample of convenience, a more definitive study with a more appropriate sample for generalizing might be conducted. Note that it is not uncommon for journals to publish reports of pilot studies, especially if they yield interesting results and point to promising directions for future research. Also note that while many researchers will explicitly identify their pilot studies as such (by using the term "pilot study"), at other times you will need to infer that a study is a pilot study from statements such as "In this preliminary study, the...."

2. Some researchers focus on *developing and testing theories*. A theory is a proposition or set of propositions that provides a cohesive explanation of the underlying dynamics of certain aspects of behavior. For example, self-verification theory indicates that people attempt to maintain stable self-concepts. Based on this theory, we can make a number of predictions. For instance, if the theory is correct, we might predict that people with poor self-concepts will seek out negative social reinforcement (e.g., seek out people who give them negative feedback about themselves) while avoiding or rejecting positive reinforcement. They do not do this because they enjoy negative reinforcement. Instead, according to the theory, it is an attempt to validate their

perceptions of themselves.[1] Such predictions can be tested with empirical research, which sheds light on the validity of a theory as well as data that may be used to further develop and refine it.

In addition to testing whether the predictions made on the basis of a theory are supported by data, researchers conduct studies to determine under what circumstances the elements of a theory hold up (e.g., In intimate relationships only? With mildly as well as severely depressed patients?). One researcher might test one aspect of the theory with a convenience sample of adolescent boys who are being treated for depression, another might test a different aspect with a convenience sample of high-achieving women, and so on. Note that they are focusing on the theory as an evolving concept rather than as a static explanation that needs to be tested with a random sample for generalization to a population. These studies may be viewed as *developmental tests* of a theory. For *preliminary* developmental work of this type, rigorous and expensive sampling from large populations usually is not justified.

3. Some researchers prefer to study a *purposive sample* rather than a random one. A purposive sample is one in which a researcher has a special interest because the individuals in a sample have characteristics that make them especially rich sources of information. For example, an anthropologist who is interested in studying tribal religious practices might purposively select a tribe that has remained isolated and, hence, may have been less influenced by outside religions than other tribes that are less isolated. Note that the tribe is not selected at random but is selected deliberately (i.e., purposively). The use of purposive samples is a tradition in *qualitative* research. (If you have not done so already, see Appendix A for a brief overview of the differences between qualitative and quantitative research.)

4. Some researchers study entire populations—not samples. This is especially true in institutional settings such as schools where all the seniors in a school district (the population) might be tested. Nevertheless, when researchers write research reports on population studies, they should describe their populations in some detail.

____ **1. Has the researcher described the sample/population in sufficient detail?**

Very satisfactory 5 4 3 2 1 Very unsatisfactory *or* N/A I/I

---

[1] For more information on this theory and its potential application to a particular behavioral issue, see Goodyear, R. K., Newcomb, M. D., & Locke. T. F. (2002). Pregnant Latina teenagers: Psychosocial and developmental determinants of how they select and perceive the men who father their children. *Journal of Counseling Psychology, 49*, 187–201. Also see Swann, Jr., W. B., Stein-Seroussi, A., & Giesler, R. B. (1992). Why people self-verify. *Journal of Personality and Social Psychology, 62*, 392–401.

Comment: As you know from the previous chapter, researchers should describe relevant demographics (i.e., background characteristics) of their participants when conducting studies in which they are generalizing from a sample to a population. This is also true when researchers are not attempting to generalize. For example, if a published pilot study shows promise for collecting meaningful data on safe-sex practices among high school students, the reader will want to know exactly what types of students were selected as participants. Were they high-achieving, articulate students? If so, the data collection procedures may not work as well with lower-achieving students. Were their parents highly educated? If so, obtaining parental permission to participate in such a study might be more difficult when the parents are less well educated. Answers to such questions are important because the role of a pilot study is to lay the groundwork for later, more definitive studies with samples more suitable for generalizing to a population.

Example 7.1.1 is drawn from a report on a developmental test of two theories. Based on each theory, a different HIV risk-reduction intervention was developed and tested in an experiment. The example shows a brief but solid description of relevant demographics of the sample. Note that the researchers were interested in conducting tests of the theories—not on generalizing to a particular population.

Example 7.1.1[2]

Detailed description of participants:

Incarcerated women ($N = 90$) were recruited from a state women's prison near a southern city with a population of approximately 400,000 and an AIDS incidence of 15.4 per 100,000 (CDC, 1995). Approximately one-third of the women were incarcerated for drug offenses and a further one-third were incarcerated for drug-related offenses (e.g., burglary to procure money for drugs). Thirteen percent (13%) reported self-injecting with needle sharing, and 25% reported using crack cocaine in the preceding year. Participants were between the ages of 17 and 53 ($M = 31.6$ years, $SD = 7.7$) and averaged 10.9 years of education ($SD = 2.4$). Household income in the preceding year was less than $10,000 per year for 85.7% of the sample and below $20,000 for 96.3%. Approximately one-third of the sample was married (35.0%), and the average number of children was 2.4 ($SD = 1.7$). Conjugal visits were allowed for the married inmates. Most of the women were African American (80.7%), and the rest were White (19.3%), consistent with the racial demographics of the prison. The mean

---

[2] St. Lawrence, J. S., Eldridge, G. D., Shelby, M. C., Little, C. E., Brasfield, T. L., & O'Bannon, R. E. (1997). HIV risk reduction for incarcerated women: A comparison of brief interventions based on two theoretical models. *Journal of Consulting and Clinical Psychology, 65,* 504–509.

number of lifetime sex partners reported was 21.6 (*SD* = 38.9; range, 0–300) and 43.8% had been treated for a sexually transmitted disease.

___ **2. For a pilot study or developmental test of a theory, has the researcher used a sample with relevant demographics?**

Very satisfactory 5 4 3 2 1 Very unsatisfactory *or* N/A I/I

Comment: Studies that often fail on this evaluation question are those in which college students are used as participants (for convenience in sampling). For example, some researchers have stretched the limits of credulity by conducting studies in which college students are asked to respond to questions that are unrelated to their life experiences, such as asking unmarried, childless college women what disciplinary measures they would take if they discovered that their hypothetical teenage sons were using illicit drugs. Obviously, this would yield little relevant information in a pilot study of a questionnaire designed for use with actual parents of teenagers.

Less extreme examples abound in the published literature such as using college students in tests of learning theories when the theories were constructed to explain the learning behavior of children. When applying this evaluation question to such studies, you should make some allowance for a "misfit" between the sample used in the pilot study (or developmental test of a theory) and the population of ultimate interest. Keep in mind that these types of studies are not designed to provide definitive data—only preliminary information that will assist in refining future research.

___ **3. Even if the purpose is not to generalize to a population, has the researcher used a sample of adequate size?**

Very satisfactory 5 4 3 2 1 Very unsatisfactory *or* N/A I/I

Comment: Very preliminary studies might be conducted using exceedingly small samples, such as trying out a questionnaire with only a handful of participants. While such studies might be useful to the researcher, their results usually are not publishable. Because there are no scientific standards for what constitutes a reasonable sample size for a pilot study to be publishable, you will need to make subjective judgments when answering this evaluation question. Likewise, there are no standards for sample sizes for developmental tests of theory.

For purposive samples, which are common in qualitative research, the sample size may be determined by the availability of participants who fit the sampling profile for the purposive sample. For instance, to study the career paths of highly achieving women in education, a researcher might decide to use female directors of statewide education agencies. If there are only a handful of such women, the sample will necessarily be limited to that number. On the other hand, when there are many potential participants who meet the standards for a purposive sample, a researcher might continue contacting additional participants until the point of "saturation," that is, the point at which additional participants are adding little new information to the picture that is emerging from the data they are collecting. In other words, new participants are revealing the same types of information as those who have already participated. Example 7.3.1 illustrates how this was described in the report of a qualitative study. Note the use of the term "data saturation" in the last sentence, which has been italicized to draw your attention to it. Using the criterion of data saturation sometimes results in the use of small samples.

Example 7.3.1[3]

A statement using "saturation" to justify the use of a small purposive sample in a qualitative study (italics added for emphasis):

Seven African American men who attended a western university were interviewed for this study. As a White man, I was unsure if African American men would have an interview with me without any prior personal contact. To address this, I was personally "vouched for" by someone the participants knew. Participants were also recruited through snowball sampling, the process of participants referring others to the researcher (Patton, 1990). Because of the depth and duration of the interviews in the present study (an average of 90 min), 7 interviewees afforded *data saturation*, the point when new data become redundant (Bogdan & Biklen, 1992).

Note that those who conduct qualitative research often have extended contact with their participants as a result of using techniques such as in-depth personal interviews or prolonged observational periods. With limited resources, their samples might necessarily be small. On the other hand, quantitative researchers often have more limited contact by using techniques such as written tests or questionnaires, which can be administered to many participants at little cost. As a result, you might expect them to use larger samples.

___ **4. If a purposive sample has been used, has the researcher indicated the basis for selecting individuals to include?**

Very satisfactory 5 4 3 2 1 Very unsatisfactory *or* N/A I/I

---

[3] Diemer, M. A. (2002). Constructions of provider role identity among African American men: An exploratory study. *Cultural Diversity and Ethnic Minority Psychology, 8,* 30–40.

Comment: Researchers should indicate the basis or criteria for the selection of a purposive sample. Example 7.4.1 is taken from a qualitative study on the workplace experiences of individuals who are HIV+ and individuals with cancer.

Example 7.4.1[4]

A description of the criteria for selecting a purposive sample for a qualitative study:

Individuals interviewed in this study were men and women who were diagnosed with HIV or cancer. Although the study focused primarily on individuals who are HIV+, the perspectives of people with cancer allowed consideration of similarities and differences in the experiences of these two groups. All participants in the study were either working at the time of the interview or had been working at some point during the prior 6 months. Participants who had cancer had to have been diagnosed within the prior 5 years to ensure that their perspective on their serious illness was current.

Note that even if a researcher calls his or her sample "purposive," usually it should be regarded as merely a sample of convenience unless the basis for its selection is described.

___ 5. If a population has been studied, has it been clearly identified and described?

Very satisfactory 5 4 3 2 1 Very unsatisfactory *or* N/A I/I

Comment: Researchers who conduct population studies often disguise the true identity of their populations (for ethical and legal reasons), especially if the results reflect negatively on the population. Nevertheless, information that helps the reader visualize the population should be given, as illustrated in Example 7.5.1. Notice that the specific city is not mentioned, but relevant information is given. Also note that "all social workers in a small city in the southeast" constitutes the population.

Example 7.5.1

Description of a population that was studied:

All social workers in a small city in the southeast were interviewed. All were college graduates, with 11% holding master's degrees while the rest

---

[4]Fesko, S. L. (2001). Workplace experiences of individuals who are HIV+ and individuals with cancer. *Rehabilitation Counseling Bulletin, 45*, 2–11.

had bachelor's degrees. The average age (median) was 39.4. The self-reported ethnicity/racial groups were White (62%), African American (30%), and "decline to state" (8%). The average salary adjusted for education and years on the job ($41,200) was slightly above the regional average.

With information such as that provided in the example, readers can make educated judgments as to whether the results are likely to apply to other populations of social workers.

___ 6. Has informed consent been obtained?

Very satisfactory   5   4   3   2   1   Very unsatisfactory   *or*   N/A   I/I

Comment: This evaluation question was raised in the previous chapter on evaluating samples when researchers generalize. (See Evaluation Question 11 in Chapter 6.) It is being raised again in this chapter because it is an important question that applies whether or not researchers are attempting to generalize.

___ 7. Overall, is the description of the sample adequate?

Very satisfactory   5   4   3   2   1   Very unsatisfactory   *or*   N/A   I/I

Comment: Rate this evaluation question after considering your answers to the earlier ones in this chapter and any additional considerations and concerns you may have.

Exercise for Chapter 7

Part A

Directions: Answer the following questions.

1. Very briefly explain in your own words how theory development might impact the selection of a sample.

2. The use of *purposive* samples is a tradition in which type of research?
   A. qualitative   B. quantitative

3. Suppose you were evaluating a research report on college students' voting

behavior. What are some demographics that you think should be described for such a study?

4. Very briefly describe in your own words the meaning of *data saturation*. Is this concept more closely affiliated with quantitative or qualitative research?

5. Which of the evaluation questions was regarded as so important that it is posed in both Chapter 6 and this chapter?

Part B

Directions: Locate several research reports of interest to you in academic journals in which the researchers are not directly concerned with generalizing from a sample to a population, and apply the evaluation questions in this chapter. Note that many qualitative researchers deliberately do *not* concern themselves with generalizability, so such reports are likely to contain descriptions that will be useful for this part of the exercise. Select the one to which you gave the highest overall rating and bring it to class for discussion. Be prepared to discuss its strengths and weaknesses.

Chapter 8

Evaluating Instrumentation

Immediately after describing the sample or population they studied, researchers almost always describe their *instruments*. An instrument is any tool or method for measuring a trait or characteristic. The description of instruments usually is identified with the subheading *Instrumentation*.[1]

Often, researchers use previously published instruments developed by others. These are easy to spot because their titles will be capitalized and references for them will be given. About equally often, researchers use instruments that they devise specifically for their particular research purposes. As a general rule, researchers should provide more information about such newly developed measures than on previously published instruments that have been described in detail in other publications, such as test manuals and other research reports.

While you would need to take several sequential courses in measurement to become an expert, you will be able to make preliminary evaluations of researchers' measurement procedures by applying the evaluation questions discussed below. Of course, your evaluations will be more definitive if you have first taken a measurement course or studied the chapter(s) on measurement in your research methods textbook.

___ **1. Have the actual items, questions, and/or directions (or at least a sample of them) been provided?**

Very satisfactory 5 4 3 2 1 Very unsatisfactory *or* N/A I/I

Comment: Providing sample items, questions, or directions is highly desirable because they help to operationalize what was measured. Note that researchers *operationalize* when they specify the physical properties of the concepts on which they are reporting.

In Example 8.1.1, the researchers used a published scale originally designed for use with health care professionals. They modified the wording of the questions to make it suitable for use with athletes, who were their participants. For each of the four burnout assessment areas, they provide a sample item. The provision of the sample items helps greatly in understanding what was measured.

---

[1] As you know from Chapter 1, *observation* is a broad term that encompasses all forms of *measurement*. The term *instrumentation* refers to the materials and tests that are used to make the observations or obtain the measurements. "Sample" and "instrumentation" are subheadings under the main heading "Method."

Example 8.1.1[2]

Portion of a description of a scale with sample questions modified for use with athletes:

Burnout was assessed [with] the Staff Burnout Scale for Health Professionals (Jones, 1980), but the words "sport," "team," or "training" were added to the items to describe the "sport" context. An example item for Cognitive Assessment is "I often think about withdrawing from sport at this level" and for Affective Assessment is "I often become angry and irritated toward my colleagues on the team." An example item for Behavioral [Assessment] is "I avoid being with my colleagues in training and competition," and for Psychophysiological Assessment is "I experience headaches while I am training...." A 6-point scale with anchors of 1: completely correct and 6: completely wrong was used....

In Example 8.1.2, the researcher provides the wording of an interview question that was posed to adults in a national survey. Notice that the term "regular household bills" is defined by giving examples. This was done to ensure that the respondents all had a common understanding of the term. Also note that by being given the actual words used in the questions, readers of the research can evaluate whether the vocabulary level is appropriate for the participants (in this case, the general adult population) as well as whether the choices are comprehensive.

Example 8.1.2[3]

Sample interview question:

In your household, who makes sure that regular household bills are paid? I mean things like the bills for gas, electricity, [and] telephone.

    1__Mainly you
    2__Mainly your husband/wife/partner
    3__Jointly with your husband/wife/partner
    4__Or someone else? [WRITE IN]

Keep in mind that many instruments are copyrighted, and their copyright holders might insist on keeping the actual items secure from public exposure. Obviously, a researcher should not be faulted for failing to provide samples when this is the case. In addition, you may want to make allowances on this evaluation question when a researcher has used a published test that is widely

---

[2] Kjormo, O., & Halvari, H. (2002). Relation of burnout with lack of time for being with significant others, role conflict, cohesion, and self-confidence among Norwegian Olympic athletes. *Perceptual and Motor Skills, 94,* 795–804.

[3] Zipp, J. F., & Toth, J. (2002). She said, he said, they said: The impact of spousal presence in survey research. *Public Opinion Quarterly, 66,* 177–208.

known and used in his or her field. Researchers who use such instruments may believe that it is not necessary to provide samples from them. Generally, the failure to supply sample items is less of a flaw when the instrument is well known than when it is newly developed.

___ **2. Are any specialized response formats, settings, and/or restrictions described in detail?**

Very satisfactory   5   4   3   2   1   Very unsatisfactory   *or*   N/A   I/I

Comment: If a researcher has provided samples of the actual items, questions, or directions, as in Examples 8.1.1 and 8.1.2 above, the response format may already be clear.

Examples of settings are the place where the measures were used (such as in the participants' homes) and whether other individuals were present (such as whether parents were present while their children were interviewed).

Examples of restrictions are time limits and tools that participants are not permitted to use (such as not permitting the use of calculators while taking a mathematics test).

Qualitative researchers also should provide details on how they collected their information even if they use loosely structured instruments such as unstructured interviews and observations. This is illustrated in Example 8.2.1 in which the setting, the length of the interviews, who was present, and other details are given for a qualitative study of children's understanding of historical change. Note that some of the photographs used during the interviews were reproduced in the journal article.

Example 8.2.1[4]
Description of data collection in a qualitative study:

[I conducted] open-ended, semistructured interviews with 121 students, aged 6–12 years, during a total of 60 interviews at the four schools. (Most students were interviewed in pairs.) In each interview, I showed students pictures from the past, asked them to arrange them in chronological order, to explain the reasons for their placements, and to estimate the approximate time period of each. I followed this task with more general questions about history. These included asking what aspects of life had changed over time and why, how people know how life was different in the past, why history is important, and where students had learned about

---

[4] Barton, K. C. (2001). A sociocultural perspective on children's understanding of historical change: Comparative findings from Northern Ireland and the United States. *American Educational Research Journal, 38*, 881–913.

the past. I frequently probed their answers or asked additional questions to follow up on issues that arose during the interviews.

___ 3. When appropriate, are multiple methods used to collect data/information on each variable?

Very satisfactory 5 4 3 2 1 Very unsatisfactory *or* N/A I/I

Comment: As you know from Chapter 1, it is safe to assume that all methods of observation (e.g., testing, interviewing) are flawed. Thus, we can have more confidence in the results of a study if more than one method for collecting the data has been used.

In quantitative research, researchers emphasize developing objective measures that meet high statistical standards for reliability and validity, which we will discuss later in this chapter. When they use these, they often do not believe that it is important to use multiple measures. For instance, they might use a well-established multiple-choice reading comprehension test that was extensively investigated (as to its validity and reliability) prior to publication of the test. A quantitative researcher would be *unlikely* to supplement this with other measures such as teachers' ratings of students' reading comprehension or some other measurement technique such as having each child read aloud and discuss what they learned from reading.

Despite their best efforts, those who construct published tests create less-than-perfect tests. Hence, using multiple measures of the same variable is desirable even if the first measure is well researched by the researchers or by a test publisher. However, it is not traditional to use multiple measures in quantitative research.

In qualitative research, researchers are more likely to use multiple measures of a single phenomenon for several reasons.[5] First, qualitative researchers strive to conduct research that is intensive and yields highly detailed results (often in the form of themes supported by verbal descriptions—as opposed to numbers). The use of multiple measures helps qualitative researchers probe more intensively from different points of view. In addition, qualitative researchers tend to view their research as exploratory; in advance of conducting exploratory research, it is difficult to know which type of measure for a particular variable is likely to be most useful. Finally, qualitative researchers see the use of multiple measures as a way to check the validity of their results. In other words, if different measures of the same phenomenon yield highly inconsistent results, the validity of the instrumentation (including the interpretation of the data) might be questioned.

---

[5] Qualitative researchers often use the term "triangulation of data sources" when they use multiple measures for the same purpose.

In Example 8.2.1 above, the researcher describes how he conducted the interviews in a qualitative study. In addition, he conducted classroom observations in the same study, as described in Example 8.3.1. Thus, he used multiple measures to study the traits of interest in his research.

Example 8.3.1[6]
Information on classroom observations in addition to interviews:

I observed most of the history lessons taught in the integrated primary school during approximately a 3-month period from September to December, for a total of 38 observations lasting about 40–50 minutes each. Combining interviews with classroom observations had the advantage of allowing comparisons of students' responses to what they had learned in class, as well as providing the chance to ask questions about the content that arose in the course of instruction.

It is not realistic to expect researchers to use multiple measures of all variables. Measurement of some variables is so straightforward that it would be poor use of a researcher's time to measure them in several ways. For instance, most researchers would be very confident in the validity of asking second-grade students to perform the one-digit multiplication facts on a paper-and-pencil test. It would be needlessly redundant to ask the students to demonstrate their achievement a second time by having an interviewer ask the same students to answer the same multiplication facts again.

___ **4. For published instruments, have sources where additional information can be obtained been cited?**

Very satisfactory 5 4 3 2 1 Very unsatisfactory *or* N/A I/I

Comment: Some instruments are "published" only in the sense that they were previously reproduced in full in journal articles. Such articles typically describe the development and statistical properties of the instruments. Other instruments are published by commercial publishers as separate publications (e.g., test booklets) that usually have accompanying manuals that describe technical information on the instruments. References to these published sources facilitate a rather detailed evaluation of instruments by those who are working intensely in an area (such as dissertation students).

In Example 8.4.1, the researchers provide two references for additional information on their instrument (indicated by the surnames and superscripts 27 and 72, which are the numbers in their reference list at the end of their journal article).

---

[6] Ibid.

Example 8.4.1[7]

The description of an instrument in which references are given:

The questionnaire used in this study is an adapted version of the California School Climate Survey (developed by Furlong and used in California) (see Furlong[27] and Rosenblatt and Furlong[72]). The research instrument had more than 100 questions pertaining to school climate, teachers' support of students, personal victimization over a range of low-level (pinching, slapping) to high-level (extortion, gun threats) violent behaviors, observed risky behaviors, and school policy regarding school violence. The original items were....

___ **5. When delving into sensitive matters, is there reason to believe that accurate data were obtained?**

Very satisfactory 5 4 3 2 1 Very unsatisfactory *or* N/A I/I

Comment: Some issues are sensitive because they deal with illegal matters such as illicit substance use, gang violence, and so on. Others are sensitive because of societal taboos such as those regarding certain forms of sexual behavior. Still others may be sensitive because of idiosyncratic personal views on privacy. For instance, age and income are sensitive issues for many individuals; participants often decline to answer these questions or may not answer honestly.

A common technique for encouraging honest answers to sensitive questions is to collect the responses anonymously. For instance, participants may be asked to mail in questionnaires with the assurance that they are not coded in any way that would reveal their identity. In group settings, participants may also be assured that their responses are anonymous, but if a group is small, such as a class of 20 students, some participants might be hesitant to be perfectly honest regarding highly sensitive matters because a small group does not provide much "cover" for hiding the identity of a participant who engages in illegal or taboo behaviors.

With techniques such as interviewing or direct physical observation, it is not possible to provide anonymity. The most a researcher might be able to do is assure *confidentiality*. Such an assurance is likely to work best if the participants already know and trust the interviewer (such as a school counselor) or if the researcher has spent enough time with the participants to develop rapport and trust. The latter is more likely to occur in qualitative research than quantitative research because qualitative researchers often spend substantial amounts of time in an effort to bond and interact with their participants.

---

[7] Astor, R. A., Benbenishty, R., Zeira, A., & Vinokur, A. (2002). School climate, observed risky behaviors, and victimization as predictors of high school students' fear and judgments of school violence as a problem. *Health Education & Behavior, 29*, 716–736.

___ **6. Have steps been taken to keep the instrumentation from obtruding on and changing any overt behaviors that were observed?**

Very satisfactory 5 4 3 2 1 Very unsatisfactory *or* N/A I/I

Comment: If participants know they are being directly observed, they may temporarily change their behavior. Clearly, this is likely to happen when studying highly sensitive behaviors, but it can also affect data collection on more ordinary matters. For instance, some students may show their best behavior if they come to class to find a newly installed video camera scanning the classroom (to gather research data); other students may show off by acting out in the presence of the camera.

One solution would be to make surreptitious observations, such as with a hidden video camera or by using a one-way mirror. In many circumstances, such techniques raise serious ethical and legal problems.

Another solution is to make the observational procedures a routine part of the research setting. For instance, if it is routine for a classroom to be visited frequently by outsiders (e.g., parents, school staff, and university observers), the presence of a researcher may be unlikely to obtrude on the behavior of the students.

___ **7. If the collection and coding of observations is highly subjective, is there evidence that similar results would be obtained if another researcher used the same measurement techniques with the same group at the same time?**

Very satisfactory 5 4 3 2 1 Very unsatisfactory *or* N/A I/I

Comment: Suppose a researcher observes groups of adolescent males interacting in various public settings, such as shopping malls, in order to collect data on aggressive behavior. Identifying some aggressive behaviors may require considerable subjectivity. If an adolescent puffs out his or her chest, is this a threatening behavior or merely a manifestation of a big sigh of relief? Is a scowl a sign of aggression or merely an expression of unhappiness? Answering such questions sometimes requires considerable subjectivity.

An important technique for addressing this issue is to have two or more independent observers make observations of the same participants at the same time. If the *rate of agreement* on the identification and classification of the behavior is reasonably high (say, 70% or more), a consumer of research will be assured that the resulting data are not idiosyncratic to one particular observer and his or her powers of observation and possible biases.

The rate of agreement is sometimes referred to as *interobserver reliability*. When the observations are reduced to scores for each participant (such as a total score for nonverbal aggressiveness), the scores based on two independent observers' observations can be expressed as an *interobserver reliability coefficient*. In reliability studies, these can range from 0.00 to 1.00, with coefficients of about 0.70 or higher indicating adequate interobserver reliability.[8]

___ **8. If an instrument is designed to measure a single unitary trait, does it have adequate internal consistency?**

Very satisfactory   5 4 3 2 1   Very unsatisfactory   *or*   N/A   I/I

Comment: A test of computational skills in mathematics at the primary grade levels measures a relatively homogeneous trait. However, a mathematics battery that measures verbal problem-solving and mathematical reasoning in addition to computational skills measures a more heterogeneous trait. Likewise, a self-report measure of depression measures a much more homogenous trait than does a measure of overall mental health.

For instruments designed to measure homogenous traits, it is important to ask whether they are *internally consistent*, that is, to what extent are the items within the instrument consistent with each other in terms of what they measure? While it is beyond the scope of this book to explain how and why it works, a statistic known as Cronbach's alpha (whose symbol is α) provides a statistical measure of internal consistency. As a special type of correlation coefficient, it ranges from 0.00 to 1.00, with values of about 0.70 or above indicating adequate internal consistency.[9] Values below this suggest that more than one trait is being measured by the instrument, which is undesirable when a researcher wants to measure only one homogenous trait. In example 8.7.1, the value of Cronbach's alpha is above the cutting point of 0.70.

Example 8.7.1[10]

Statement regarding internal consistency using "Cronbach's alpha":

Parental discipline (Parental Attitudes toward Childrearing Scale, Easterbrooks & Goldberg, 1984), a 20-item measure…reflected mothers'

---

[8] Mathematically, these coefficients are the same as *correlation coefficients*, which are covered in all standard introductory statistics courses. You may know that correlation coefficients can range from –1.00 to 1.00, with a value of 0.00 indicating no relationship. In practice, however, negatives are not found in reliability studies.

[9] *Split-half reliability* also measures internal consistency, but Cronbach's alpha is widely considered a superior measure. Hence, split-half reliability is seldom reported. Should you encounter it, it will be expressed as a coefficient with values of about 0.70 and above being considered satisfactory.

[10] Mowbray, C., Oyserman, D., Bybee, D., & MacFarlane, P. (2002). Parenting of mothers with a serious mental illness: Differential effects of diagnosis, clinical history, and other mental health variables. *Social Work Research*, 26, 225–240.

self-reports of strictness of discipline practices and structure in child management ($M = 3.45$, $SD = .50$, Cronbach's alpha = .75).

Internal consistency usually is regarded as an issue only when an instrument is designed to measure a single homogeneous trait *and* when the instrument yields scores (as opposed to instruments such as interviews when used to identify patterns that are described in words). If an instrument does not meet these two criteria, you should answer "not applicable" to this evaluation question.

___ 9. For stable traits, is there evidence of temporal stability?

Very satisfactory   5   4   3   2   1   Very unsatisfactory   *or*   N/A   I/I

Comment: Suppose a researcher wants to measure aptitude (i.e., potential) for learning algebra. Such an aptitude is widely regarded as being stable. In other words, it is unlikely to fluctuate much from one week or even one year to another without additional mathematics instruction. Hence, a test of such an aptitude should yield results that are stable across at least short periods of time. To put it more concretely, if a student's score on such a test administered this week indicates that he or she has very little aptitude for learning algebra, this test should yield a similar assessment if administered to the same student next week.

Although it is a little harder to see in the area of personality measurement, most measures of personality also should yield results that have temporal stability (i.e., are stable over time). For example, suppose a researcher wants to measure the deep-seated, long-term self-esteem of participants. While self-esteem may fluctuate modestly over even short periods of time, a researcher usually does *not* want a measure that is overly sensitive to such temporary fluctuations. Hence, he or she would want to use a measure that yields scores that are similar from one week or one month to another.

The most straightforward approach to assessing temporal stability is to administer the instrument to a group of participants twice at different points in time—typically with a couple of weeks between administrations, although sometimes it is examined over a more extended period of time. The two sets of scores can be correlated, and if a coefficient (whose symbol is *r*) of about 0.70 or more (on a scale from 0.00 to 1.00) is obtained, there is evidence of temporal stability. This type of reliability is commonly known as *test-retest reliability*. As its name implies, this type of reliability is usually examined only when *tests* or scales that yield scores are used in research.

While temporal stability is an important issue, it usually is addressed in research reports mainly when researchers use previously published instruments that have been extensively studied. Unfortunately, researchers seldom examine temporal stability when using newly developed instruments in a particular study on which they are reporting, since establishing temporal reliability would constitute a study in and of itself. However, there are exceptions. Example 8.9.1 illustrates how researchers describe how they established the test-retest reliability of their instrument. Note that they use the symbol *r* and report a value well above the suggested cutting point of 0.70.

Example 8.9.1[11]

Statement regarding temporal stability (test-retest reliability):

This inventory [designed to measure literacy] was piloted on a group of 50 students who did not attend any of the 10 schools in this study and were not considered part of this study. The test-retest reliability was *r* = .82.

___ 10. When appropriate, is there evidence of content validity?

Very satisfactory   5   4   3   2   1   Very unsatisfactory   *or*   N/A   I/I

Comment: An important issue in the evaluation of achievement tests is the extent to which the contents of the tests (i.e., the stimulus materials and skills) are suitable in light of the research purpose. For instance, if a researcher has used an achievement test to study the extent to which the second graders in a school district have achieved the skills expected of them at this grade level, an evaluator of the research will want to know whether the contents of the test are aligned with (or match) the contents of the second-grade curriculum.

While content validity is most closely associated with measurement of achievement, it also is sometimes used as a construct for evaluating other types of measures. For instance, a researcher might point out that the contents of a scale designed to measure depression correspond to a list of traits associated with depression outlined in a widely accepted diagnostic manual on psychological disorders. Such a match assures readers of the research that the measure of depression represents mainstream thinking regarding this trait.[12]

___ 11. When appropriate, is there evidence of empirical validity?

Very satisfactory   5   4   3   2   1   Very unsatisfactory   *or*   N/A   I/I

Comment: Empirical validity refers to validity established by collecting data using the instrument in order to determine the extent to which the data "make

---

[11] Fisher, D., Lapp, D., & Flood, J. (2001). The effects of access to print through the use of community libraries on the reading performance of elementary students. *Reading Improvement, 38*, 175–182.

[12] Of course, some researchers deviate from the mainstream on certain measurement issues. There is nothing inherently wrong with this as long as the deviation(s) are clearly described and a rationale is given for them.

sense." For instance, a depression scale might be empirically validated by administering it to an institutionalized, clinically depressed group of adult patients as well as to a random sample of adult patients visiting family physicians for annual checkups. We would expect that the scores of the two groups will differ substantially in a predicted direction (i.e., the institutionalized sample should have higher depression scores). If not, the validity of the scale would be quite questionable.

Sometimes the empirical validity of a test is expressed with a correlation coefficient. For example, a test maker might correlate scores on the College Board's SAT with freshman grades in college. A correlation of .40 or more might be interpreted as indicating the test has validity as a modest predictor of college grades.

Empirical validity comes in many forms, and a full exploration of it would require a book of its own. Some key terms that suggest that empirical validity has been explored are *predictive validity, concurrent validity, criterion-related validity, discriminate validity, construct validity*, and *factor analysis*.

If you are new to the field of research and measurement, you may feel at this point that you would be hopelessly lost in trying to evaluate instruments in light of this evaluation question. However, even without formal training in measurement, you can check to see whether a researcher has addressed this issue. When researchers do this, they usually only briefly summarize the information, and these summaries are usually comprehensible to those who are new to the field. Examples 8.11.1 and 8.11.2 illustrate fairly typical summaries. Notice that they are exceptionally brief but contain references to publications where additional information may be obtained.

Example 8.11.1[13]

Statement regarding empirical validity of an instrument with a reference to its test manual[14] where more information may be obtained:

The Test of Early Reading Ability-2 (TERS-2) (Reid, Hresko, & Hammill, 1989) is a norm-referenced assessment instrument.... The authors reported adequate construct validity including significant correlations (.61) with performance on the Basic Skills Inventory-Diagnostic Reading Subtest, high correlations with chronological age and school experience (.84), and successful differentiation of normal and learning-disabled students.

---

[13] Sacks, C. H., & Mergendoller, J. R. (1997). The relationship between teachers' theoretical orientation toward reading and student outcomes in kindergarten children with different initial reading abilities. *American Educational Research Journal, 34*, 721–739.

[14] Note that the reference to Reid, Hresko, & Hammill, 1989, is a reference to the manual for the test.

Example 8.11.2[15]

Statement regarding empirical validity of an instrument with a reference to where more information may be obtained:

To assess binge drinking, we asked participants to respond either "yes" (= 1) or "no" (= 2) to the question "Have you had five or more drinks at any one time during the past three months?" This item has demonstrated very good validity in past studies (e.g., Taj, Devera-Sales, & Vinson, 1998).

Unfortunately, empirical validity is seldom addressed when researchers use newly developed instruments devised for their specific research studies. This is because an adequate empirical validity study is a major study in and of itself.

Note that it is traditional for researchers to address empirical validity only for instruments that yield scores, as opposed to instruments such as semistructured interviews.

___ 12. Is the instrumentation adequate in light of the research purpose?

Very satisfactory   5   4   3   2   1   Very unsatisfactory   *or*   N/A   I/I

Comment: One of the most important considerations when evaluating instrumentation is whether it is appropriate in light of a researcher's purpose for conducting a study. Is there a match between what the researcher needs to measure to achieve his or her purpose and the instrument he or she used?

Careful researchers attempt to show their readers that they have selected instruments appropriate for achieving their research objectives. Often, they will discuss why a particular instrument was chosen over others or how an instrument was modified to make it more suitable to the research purpose.

___ 13. Overall, is the instrumentation adequate?

Very satisfactory   5   4   3   2   1   Very unsatisfactory   *or*   N/A   I/I

Comment: The amount of information about instruments used in research that is reported in academic journals is often quite limited. The provision of references for obtaining additional information helps to overcome this common flaw.

In reaching your overall evaluation, you should usually place more emphasis on Evaluation Question 12 (Is the instrumentation adequate in light of the research purpose?) than on the other questions. You should do this because

---

[15] Wiscott, R., Kopera-Frye, K., & Begovic, A. (2002). Binge drinking in later life: Comparing young–old and old–old drinkers. *Psychology of Addictive Behaviors, 16*, 252–255.

an instrument that passes muster on all the other questions but fails Evaluation Question 12 is invalid for use in the particular research you are considering. For example, if a researcher needs to measure reading comprehension to achieve his or her research purpose, but for the sake of expediency uses a test that is known to be a highly valid and reliable measure of vocabulary knowledge (one limited aspect of reading comprehension), the test has limited validity *for this particular research purpose.* In other words, validity is relative to the purpose for which an instrument is being used. It might be highly valid for one purpose but have limited validity for another. Likewise, it is relative to the backgrounds of the participants. For example, a measure that works well with children might have less validity with adults.

Generally speaking, if a researcher provides too little information for you to make an informed judgment, you should give it a low rating on this evaluation question or respond that there is "insufficient information" (I/I). When considering instruments used in research, an I/I indicates an important flaw in the research.

Exercise for Chapter 8

Part A

Directions: Answer the following questions.

1. Consider Example 8.2.1. In your opinion, does it provide sufficient detail? If no, briefly describe other details you think consumers of research would want to know.

2. Very briefly name three reasons why qualitative researchers tend to use multiple measures (such as interviews supplemented by observations).

3. Name two or three issues that some participants might regard as sensitive and, hence, difficult to measure. Answer this question with examples that are *not* mentioned in this book. (See the discussion of Evaluation Question 5.)

4. Have you ever changed your behavior because you knew (or thought) you were being observed? If yes, briefly describe how or why you were being observed and what behavior(s) you changed. (See Evaluation Question 6.)

5. According to this chapter, what is a reasonably high rate of agreement when two or more independent observers classify behavior?

6. For which of the following would it be more important to look at internal consistency using Cronbach's alpha? Explain your answer.

    A. For a single test of mathematics ability for first graders that yields a single score.

    B. For a single test of reading and mathematics abilities for first graders that yields a single score.

7. Suppose a researcher obtained a test-retest reliability coefficient of 0.86. According to this chapter, does this indicate adequate temporal stability? Explain.

8. Which type of validity is mentioned in this chapter as being an important issue in the evaluation of achievement tests?

9. According to this chapter, when making an overall evaluation of an instrument used by a researcher, which one of the evaluation questions should receive the most emphasis?

Part B

Directions: Locate several research reports of interest to you in academic journals. Evaluate the descriptions of the instruments in light of the evaluation questions in this chapter as well as any other considerations and concerns you may have. Select the one to which you gave the highest overall rating, and bring it to class for discussion. Be prepared to discuss both its strengths and weaknesses.

Chapter 9

Evaluating Experimental Procedures

An experiment is a study in which treatments are given in order to determine their effects. For example, we might train one group of children how to use conflict-resolution techniques (the experimental group) and compare them with another group of children who are not trained (the control group). Following this, we could observe all the children on the playground to determine whether the experimental group used more conflict-resolution techniques than the control group did.

The treatments (training versus no training) constitute what is known as the *independent variable*, which can be thought of as the stimulus or input variable. The resulting behavior on the playground constitutes the *dependent variable*, which can be thought of as the output or response variable.

You will be able to identify experiments because any study in which even a single treatment is given to just a single participant is an experiment as long as the purpose of the study is to determine the effects of the treatment on another variable. A study that does not meet this minimal condition is *not* an experiment. Thus, for example, a political poll in which questions are asked but no treatments are given is not an experiment and should not be referred to as such.

The following evaluation questions cover only the most important principles for the evaluation of experiments. To a large extent, the presentation is nontechnical. To become conversant with the technical terms and jargon associated with experimentation, consult any major research methods textbook.

___ **1. If two or more groups are compared, were individuals assigned at random to the groups?**

Very satisfactory 5 4 3 2 1 Very unsatisfactory *or* N/A I/I

Comment: By assigning individuals at random to the groups, we are assured that there is no bias in the assignment. For instance, random assignment to two groups in the experiment on conflict-resolution training (mentioned at the beginning of this chapter) assures us that there is no bias, such as systematically assigning the less aggressive children to the experimental group. It is *not* safe to assume the assignment was done at random unless a researcher explicitly states that it was done, which is illustrated in Example 9.1.1. Note that after the random assignment, repeated attempts were made to obtain the continuing participation of those assigned to the two experimental groups.

Example 9.1.1[1]

Excerpt from an experiment with random assignment explicitly mentioned:

Once consent was obtained, the client completed the baseline assessment. Following the baseline assessment, clients were randomly assigned to one of the three…intervention conditions: role induction (RI), motivational interview (MI), or the no-intervention control group (CG). Clients assigned to either the RI or MI condition were scheduled for an appointment with a therapist who conducted the assigned intervention. If necessary, repeated attempts were made to reschedule any client in the RI or MI conditions who cancelled or failed to appear for his or her intervention session appointment.

Note that assigning *individuals* to treatments at random is vastly superior to assigning previously existing *groups* to treatments at random. For example, in educational research, it is not uncommon to assign one class to an experimental treatment and another class to serve as the control group. Because students are not ordinarily randomly assigned to classes, there may be systematic differences between the two classes. School principals and counselors use various criteria and considerations in making class assignments, and these can be presumed to lead to the creation of groups that are systematically different. Thus, you should *not* answer "yes" to this evaluation question unless *individuals* were assigned at random.

If you can answer "yes" to this evaluation question, the experiment you are evaluating is known as a *true experiment*. Note that this term does not imply that the experiment is perfect, as you will see when you apply some of the other evaluation questions in this chapter. In other words, a *true experiment* has the very desirable characteristic of having individuals assigned to treatment and control conditions at random. The term does not refer to other aspects of an experiment.

___ **2. If two or more comparison groups were *not* formed at random, is there evidence that they were initially equal in important ways?**

Very satisfactory   5   4   3   2   1   Very unsatisfactory   *or*   N/A   I/I

Comment: Suppose a researcher wants to study the impact of a new third-grade

---

[1] Connors, G. J., Walitzer, K. S., & Dermen, K. H. (2002). Preparing clients for alcoholism treatment: Effects on treatment participation and outcomes. *Journal of Consulting and Clinical Psychology, 70*, 1161–1169.

reading program that is being used with all third graders in a school (the experimental group). To get a control group, the researcher will have to use third graders in another school.[2] Because students are not randomly assigned to schools, this experiment will get low marks on Evaluation Question 1. However, if the researcher selects a control school in which the first graders have standardized test scores similar to those in the experimental school and are similar in other important respects such as parents' socioeconomic status, some useful information may still be obtained.

Note, however, that having such evidence of similarity between groups is not as satisfactory as assigning individuals at random to groups. For example, the children in the two schools in our example may be different in some important respect that the researcher has overlooked. Perhaps the children's parents in the experimental school are more involved in their children's schooling than the parents in the other school. This involvement, rather than the new reading program, might be the cause of any differences in reading achievement between the two groups.

When using two intact groups (such as two schools), it is important to give both a pretest and a posttest to measure the dependent variable. For instance, to evaluate the reading program, a researcher should give a pretest in reading, which will establish whether the two intact groups are initially similar on the dependent variable. Of course, the experiment will be more interpretable if they are initially similar.[3]

___ 3. If only a single participant or a single group is used, have the treatments been alternated?

Very satisfactory   5   4   3   2   1   Very unsatisfactory   *or*   N/A   I/I

Comment: Not all experiments involve the comparison of groups that have been treated differently. Consider, for example, a teacher who wants to try using increased praise for appropriate behaviors in the classroom to see if it reduces behaviors such as inappropriate out-of-seat behavior (IOSB). To conduct an experiment on this, the teacher could count the number of IOSBs for a week or two before administering the increased praise. This would yield what is called the *baseline data*. Suppose the teacher then introduces the extra praise and finds a decrease in the IOSBs. This might suggest that the extra praise *caused* the

---

[2] As you may know, the use of two intact groups (groups that were already formed) with both a pretest and a posttest is known as a *quasi-experiment*—as opposed to a *true experiment*.

[3] If the groups are initially dissimilar, a researcher should consider locating another group that is more similar to serve as the control. If this is not possible, a statistical technique known as analysis of covariance can be used to adjust the posttest scores in light of the initial differences in pretest scores. Such a statistical adjustment can be risky if the assumptions underlying the test have been violated, a topic beyond the scope of this book.

improvement. However, such a conclusion would be highly tenuous because children's environments are constantly changing in many ways and some other environmental influence (such as the school principal scolding the students on the playground without the teacher's knowledge) might be the real cause of the change. A more definitive test would be for the teacher to reverse the treatment and go back to giving less praise, followed by another reversal to the higher praise condition. If the data form the expected pattern, the teacher would have reasonable evidence that increased praise reduces IOSB.

Notice that in this type of experiment, the single group serves as a control during the baseline, serves as the experimental group when the extra praise is initially given, serves as the control again when the condition is reversed, and finally serves as the experimental group again when the extra praise is reintroduced. Such a design has this strength: The same children with the same backgrounds are both the experimental and control groups. (In a two-group experiment, the children in one group may be different from the children in the other group in some important way that affects the outcome of the experiment.) The major drawback of a single group design is that the same children are being exposed to multiple treatments, which may lead to unnatural reactions. How does a child feel when some weeks he or she gets extra praise for appropriate behaviors but other weeks does not? Obviously, such reactions could confound the experiment.

If two classes were available for an experiment of the type we are considering, a teacher could use a *multiple baseline design*, in which the initial extra praise condition is started on a different week for each group. If the pattern of decreased IOSB under the extra praise condition holds up across both groups, the causal conclusion would be even stronger than when only one group was used at one point in time.

The type of experimentation being discussed under this evaluation question is often referred to as *single-subject research* or *behavior analysis*. When a professional has only a single participant or intact group that cannot be divided at random into two or more groups, such a design can provide useful information about causality.

___ 4. Are the treatments described in sufficient detail?

Very satisfactory 5 4 3 2 1 Very unsatisfactory *or* N/A I/I

Comment: Researchers should give rather thorough descriptions of the treatments that were administered since the sole purpose of an experiment is to estimate the effects of the treatments on dependent variables. The reader should be able to picture what was done and by whom. If the treatments are complex, such as two types of therapy in clinical psychology applied for an extended period of time, researchers should give references to additional publications where detailed accounts can be found, if possible.

___ 5. If the treatments were administered by individuals other than the researcher, were they properly trained?

Very satisfactory 5 4 3 2 1 Very unsatisfactory *or* N/A I/I

Comment: Researchers often rely on other individuals, such as graduate assistants, teachers, and psychologists, to administer the treatments they are using in an experiment. When this is the case, it is desirable for the researcher to assure the readers that they were properly trained. Otherwise, it is possible that the treatments were modified in some unknown way. Example 9.5.1 shows a statement regarding the training of three assistants who administered three types of training (the treatments). Hence, *training the trainers* refers to training those conducting the experimental training. Note that such statements are typically brief.

Example 9.5.1[4]

Excerpt on training those who administered the treatments:

Training the trainers. Scripts of the training sessions for the three conditions (recall, skills, and counseling education) were developed and critiqued by all four authors. The three trainers then met and practiced until they felt comfortable with the content of each session and assured that they could conduct each session effectively and consistently.

___ 6. If the treatments were administered by individuals other than the researcher, was there a check to see if they administered the treatments properly?

Very satisfactory 5 4 3 2 1 Very unsatisfactory *or* N/A I/I

Comment: Even if those who administered the treatments were trained, they normally should be monitored. This is especially true for long and complex treatment cycles. For instance, if psychologists will be trying out new techniques with clients over a period of several months, it would be desirable to spot-check their efforts to determine whether they are applying their training properly. This can be done by directly observing them or by questioning them.

---

[4] Rochlen, A. B., Ligiero, D. P., Hill, C. E., & Heaton, K. J. (1999). Effects of training in dream recall and dream interpretation skills on dream recall, attitudes, and dream interpretation outcome. *Journal of Counseling Psychology*, 46, 27–34.

___ **7. If each treatment group had a different person administering a treatment, has the researcher tried to eliminate the "personal effect"?**

Very satisfactory   5   4   3   2   1   Very unsatisfactory   *or*   N/A   I/I

Comment: Suppose that the purpose of an experiment is to compare the effectiveness of three methods for teaching decoding skills in first-grade reading instruction. If each method is used by a different teacher, differences in the teachers (such as ability to build rapport with students, level of enthusiasm, ability to build effective relationships with parents) may cause any observed differences in achievement (i.e, they may have had a "personal effect" on the outcome). One solution to this problem is to have each of the three methods used by a large number of teachers, with the teachers assigned at random to the methods. If such a large-scale study is not possible, another solution is to have each teacher use all three methods. In other words, Teacher A could use Methods X, Y, and Z at different points in time with different children; the other two teachers would do likewise. When the results are averaged, the "personal effect" of each teacher will have contributed to the average scores earned under each of the three methods.

___ **8. Except for differences in the treatments, were all other conditions the same in the experimental and control groups?**

Very satisfactory   5   4   3   2   1   Very unsatisfactory   *or*   N/A   I/I

Comment: The results of an experiment can be influenced by many variables other than the independent variable. For instance, if experimental and control groups are treated at different times of the day or in different rooms in a building (where one room is noisy and the other is not), these factors might influence the outcome of an experiment. We say that variables such as these are *confounding variables* because they confound the interpretation.

Many researchers are silent on whether all other conditions were controlled by making them the same for all groups in an experiment. Undoubtedly, many of them believe that readers will assume that the researcher is aware of this requirement for a good experiment and has met it without having to discuss it. In other cases, you may have some legitimate concerns about this issue. For example, if a researcher tells you that the experimental treatment was administered to children in one teacher's class while the children in another teacher's class served as controls, you may have concerns about the comparability of the two teachers' classrooms.

___ 9. If necessary, did the researchers disguise the purpose of the experiment from the participants?

Very satisfactory 5 4 3 2 1 Very unsatisfactory *or* N/A I/I

Comment: If participants know the true, exact purpose of an experiment, their responses may be influenced by this knowledge. For example, in a study on the effects of a film showing negative consequences of drinking alcohol, the experimental group participants might report more negative attitudes toward alcohol simply because they know the researcher has hypothesized that this will happen. In other words, sometimes participants try to give researchers what they think the researchers expect. This is known as a *demand characteristic*. It is called this because it is as though a researcher is subtly demanding a certain outcome.

Certain types of instruments are more prone to the effects of demand characteristics than others. Self-report measures (such as self-reported attitudes toward alcohol) are especially sensitive to them. On the other hand, an achievement test is less sensitive because a student who does not have the skills being tested will not be successful on the test even if he or she is trying to please the researcher. Likewise, many physical measures are insensitive to this type of influence. In an experiment on methods for reducing HIV, for instance, a subject will not be able to alter the results of a blood test for HIV.

Example 9.9.1 shows how a researcher attempted to blunt knowledge of the expected experimental outcome.

Example 9.9.1[5]

Excerpt on disguising the purpose of an experiment:

After watching the film, participants were asked to fill out a questionnaire containing questions for measuring alcohol-related attitudes, preceded by some unrelated items that were intended to keep them from getting to know the research purpose.

In Example 9.9.2, the experimenter wanted to measure attitudes toward residents of Newfoundland (a province in Canada whose residents are sometimes made fun of by other Canadians). It seemed better to disguise this true purpose by indicating that it was a study of perceptions people have of Canadians from all provinces and make it seem as though each participant just happened to draw Newfoundland as a province to which to react.

---

[5] Bahk, C. M. (1997). The impact of presence versus absence of negative consequences in dramatic portrayals of alcohol drinking. *Journal of Alcohol and Drug Education, 42*, 18–26.

Example 9.9.2[6]

Excerpt on disguising the purpose of an experiment:

[The participants] were told that because of time constraints, it would not be possible to ask each participant about every province. Consequently, each participant was asked to randomly draw a province from a cup. (All slips in the cup were labeled "Newfoundland.")

Although it is sometimes desirable to deceive participants (at least temporarily) for methodological reasons, this can raise ethical issues that a researcher would want to consider carefully. Most colleges and universities have review boards that can provide input on this matter.

___ 10. Is the setting for the experiment "natural"?

Very satisfactory   5   4   3   2   1   Very unsatisfactory   *or*   N/A   I/I

Comment: Sometimes researchers conduct experiments in unnatural settings. When they do this, they limit their study's *external validity*, that is, what is found in the unnatural environment of a study may not be found in more natural settings (i.e., the finding may not be valid in a more natural setting).

Experiments conducted in laboratory settings often have poor external validity. Notice the unnatural aspects of Example 9.10.1. First, the amount and type of alcoholic beverages were assigned. Second, the female was a cohort of the experimenter (not someone the males were actually dating). Third, the setting was a laboratory, where the males would be likely to suspect that their behavior was being monitored in some way. While the researchers have achieved a high degree of control over the experiment, they have sacrificed external validity in the process.

Example 9.10.1

Experiment with poor external validity:

A research team was interested in the effects of alcohol consumption on aggressiveness in males when dating. In their experiment, some of the males were given moderate amounts of beer to consume. Then all males were observed interacting with a female cohort of the experimenters. The interactions took place in a laboratory on a college campus, and observations were made through a one-way mirror.

---

[6] Maio, G. R., Olson, J. M., & Bush, J. (1997). Telling jokes that disparage social groups: Effects on the joke teller's stereotypes. *Journal of Applied Social Psychology, 27,* 1986–2000.

____ **11. Has the researcher distinguished between *random selection* and *random assignment*?**

Very satisfactory 5 4 3 2 1 Very unsatisfactory *or* N/A I/I

Comment: The desirability of using *random selection* to obtain samples from which we can generalize with confidence to larger populations was discussed in Chapter 6. Such selection is highly desirable in any study—whether it is an experiment or not. *Random assignment*, on the other hand, refers to the process for assigning participants to the various treatment conditions (i.e., to the treatments, including any control condition).

Note that in any given experiment, *selection* may or may not be random. Likewise, *assignment* may or may not be random. Figure 9.11.1 illustrates the ideal situation where first there is random selection from a population of interest to obtain a sample. This is followed by random assignment of individuals to treatment conditions.

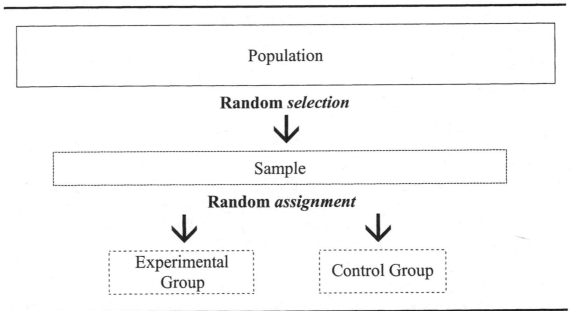

Figure 9.11.1.   Ideal combination of random selection and random assignment.

When discussing the generalizability of the results of an experiment, a researcher should do so in light of the type of *selection* used. In other words, a properly selected sample (ideally, selected at random) allows for more confidence when generalizing the results to a population. On the other hand, when discussing the comparability of the two groups, a researcher should consider the type of *assignment* used. In other words, proper assignment to a group (ideally, assigned at random) increases our confidence that the two groups were initially equal—permitting a valid comparison of the outcomes of treatments and control conditions.

___ **12. Has the researcher used ethical and politically acceptable treatments?**

Very satisfactory 5 4 3 2 1 Very unsatisfactory *or* N/A I/I

Comment: This evaluation question is applicable primarily to experiments in applied areas such as education, clinical psychology, social work, and medicine. For example, has the researcher used treatments to promote classroom discipline that will be acceptable to parents, teachers, and the community? Or, has the researcher used methods such as moderate corporal punishment by teachers, which will probably be unacceptable to many people?

A low mark on this question means that the experiment is unlikely to have an impact in the applied area in which it was conducted.

___ **13. Overall, was the experiment properly conducted?**

Very satisfactory 5 4 3 2 1 Very unsatisfactory *or* N/A I/I

Comment: Rate the overall quality of the experimental procedures based on the answers to the evaluation questions in this chapter and any other concerns you may have.

Concluding Comment

This chapter presents a commonsense approach to the evaluation of experiments. For those of you who are using this book in coordination with a traditional research methods textbook, a few comments on terminology are in order. First, most textbooks distinguish between *internal validity* and *external validity*. We say that an experiment has high *internal validity* when the differences in treatment are the only logical possible cause for any observed differences among groups. Evaluation Questions 1 through 8 in this chapter deal with this issue. On the other hand, we say that an experiment has high *external validity* when we have confidence that the results apply to the population to which the researcher wishes to generalize. Evaluation Questions 9 through 11 deal with this second issue. Evaluation Question 11 deals with both these issues because *random selection* contributes to a study's external validity while *random assignment* contributes to its internal validity.

As a final matter, an experiment to which participants are assigned at random is said to be a *true experiment*. An experiment in which groups are formed in a nonrandom fashion but on which we have data suggesting that they are initially equal is said to be a *quasi-experiment*.[7] Experiments of lesser quality (such as not having a control condition or comparing two groups that are not formed at random and for which we have no data on their initial equality) are said to be *pre-experiments*.

Exercise for Chapter 9

Part A

Directions: Answer the following questions.

1. In an experiment, the treatments constitute what is known as
    A. an independent variable.   B. a dependent variable.

2. Which of the following is described in this chapter as being vastly superior to the other?
    A. Assigning previously existing *groups* to treatments at random.
    B. Assigning *individuals* to treatments at random.

3. Suppose a psychology professor conducted an experiment in which one of her sections of Introduction to Social Psychology was assigned to be the experimental group and the other section served as the control group during a given semester. The experimental group used computer-assisted instruction while the control group received instruction via a traditional lecture/discussion method. Although both groups are taking a course in social psychology during the same semester, the two groups might be initially different in other ways. Speculate on what some of the differences might be. (See Evaluation Question 2.)

4. In this chapter, what is described as a strength of an experimental design in which one group serves as both the treatment group and its own control group?

5. Very briefly describe how the "personal effect" might confound an experiment.

6. In your opinion, is it ethical to disguise the purpose of an experiment from participants? Do Examples 9.9.1 and 9.9.2 concern you from an ethical point of view? Explain.

---

[7] Quasi-experimental designs include single-subject/behavior analysis designs that have reversals (see Evaluation Question 3). These are not true experiments, by definition, because they do not include random assignment of individuals to groups.

7. Explain what it means to say that a particular experiment lacks *external validity*.

8. Briefly explain how *random selection* differs from *random assignment*.

9. Is it possible to have *nonrandom selection* yet still have *random assignment* in an experiment? Explain.

Part B

Directions: Locate several experiments on topics of interest to you in academic journals. Evaluate them in light of the evaluation questions in this chapter as well as any other considerations and concerns you may have. Select the one to which you gave the highest overall rating and bring it to class for discussion. Be prepared to discuss both its strengths and weaknesses.

Chapter 10

Evaluating Results Sections

In quantitative reports, the results section almost always contains statistics that summarize the data that were collected and describes the results of significance testing. In qualitative reports, the results section consists of a description of themes and trends, frequently supplemented with quotations (often called "verbatims") from participants or descriptions of overt behaviors that were observed.

In this chapter, it is assumed that you have basic knowledge of elementary statistical methods.

___ **1. Is the results section a cohesive essay?**

Very satisfactory 5 4 3 2 1 Very unsatisfactory *or* N/A I/I

Comment: The results section should be an essay—not just a collection of statistics or quotations from participants. In other words, researchers should describe results in paragraphs, each of which describes some aspect of the results. These paragraphs usually will contain statistics (when a study is quantitative), but the gist of the results should be clear even if one ignores the statistics. This is illustrated in Example 10.1.1, where the words describe the major results, which are supported by statistics. Also notice the use of the transitional term "however," which signals this anomaly in the results: While the non-Asians were more confident, they scored lower. The researchers, quite correctly, are guiding their readers through the results—not just letting the statistics speak for themselves.

Example 10.1.1[1]
Main ideas expressed in words, supported by statistics from a quantitative study:

Regarding self-efficacy beliefs, non-Asian students appeared more confident with their abilities to accomplish the verbal tasks by reporting higher levels of self-efficacy beliefs ($M = 3.02$ out of 4; $SD = .67$, $t = 2.25$, $p < .05$). However, Asian American students out-performed their non-

---

[1] Eaton, M. J., & Dembo, M. H. (1997). Differences in the motivational beliefs of Asian American and non-Asian students. *Journal of Educational Psychology, 89*, 433–440.

Asian counterparts by scoring approximately 90% on the achievement assessment, whereas the non-Asian students scored approximately 75%.

The results section of qualitative studies also should be presented as a cohesive essay. Example 10.1.2 shows the beginning of a results section of a report of a qualitative study. Notice that the researchers use the first paragraph to describe the organization of their results section. Such a paragraph is highly desirable when the results are extensive.

Example 10.1.2[2]

Description of the organization of results from a qualitative study:

Analysis of the participants' interviews generated a variety of categories, with some variation occurring between the participants who had attended or completed college and those who had attended or completed high school. Within two domains—meaning of career and success are a collective experience—the categories were consistent across the entire sample, with educational level appearing to make no difference in the participants' beliefs and experiences. For the remaining three domains—supportive factors, obstacles, and living in two worlds—unique categories emerged between the two groups. The results presented below are organized around the domains. Categories that arose in fewer than three cases were dropped from further consideration, as they were not considered sufficiently stable.

Meaning of Career

Three categories emerged from participant responses to the "grand tour" question (McCracken, 1988, as cited in Hill et al., 1997) "What does career mean to you?" (see Table 1). The participants typically identified a career as being a lifelong endeavor....

___ 2. Does the researcher refer back to the research hypotheses, purposes, or questions originally stated in the introduction?

Very satisfactory 5 4 3 2 1 Very unsatisfactory *or* N/A I/I

Comment: This evaluation question may not be applicable to a very short research report with a single hypothesis, question, or purpose. When there are several of these, however, readers should be shown how different elements of the results relate to the specific hypotheses, questions, or purposes, as illustrated

---

[2] Juntunen, C. L. et al. (2001). American Indian perspectives on the career journey. *Journal of Counseling Psychology, 48*, 274–285.

in Example 10.2.1. The authors of this example had three hypotheses and refer to them by their ordinal position ("1," "2," and "3"). They also indicate the content of each hypothesis (e.g., Hypothesis 3: The women shown in the photos were viewed as less feminine when described as entrepreneurs than as managers).

Example 10.2.1[3]

Results discussed in terms of specific hypotheses:

Results offered support for Hypotheses 1 and 2; as predicted, women shown in standard-format photos received higher ratings when they were described as being entrepreneurs than when they were described as being managers. This pattern was obtained both for personal traits (Hypothesis 1) and for the perceived causes of their success (i.e., attributions–Hypothesis 2).… In more specific terms, the women were rated significantly higher on two traits—decisiveness and career seriousness—when described as entrepreneurs (Hypothesis 1). Similarly, their success was attributed less to luck and more to specific skills (i.e., social skills–Hypothesis 2). Finally, as predicted by Hypothesis 3, the women shown in the photos were viewed as less feminine when described as entrepreneurs than as managers.

___ **3. Are the results of *qualitative* studies adequately supported with examples of quotations or descriptions of observations?**

Very satisfactory   5   4   3   2   1   Very unsatisfactory   *or*   N/A   I/I

Comment: Qualitative researchers typically report few, if any, statistics in the results section. Instead, they tend to report on what themes and categories emerged, often looking for patterns that might have implications for theory development. Instead of statistics, quotations from participants or descriptions of observations of the participants' behavior are used to support the general statements regarding results. This is illustrated in Example 10.3.1, in which the actual words of two participants are reported to support a finding.

Example 10.3.1[4]

Results of a qualitative study supported by examples:

The participants typically identified a career as being a lifelong endeavor, with 16 of the 18 participants expressing the view that career is a

---

[3] Baron, R. A., Markman, G. D., & Hirsa, A. (2001). Perceptions of women and men as entrepreneurs: Evidence for differential effects of attributional augmenting. *Journal of Applied Psychology, 86,* 923–929.
[4] Juntunen, C. L. et al. (2001). American Indian perspectives on the career journey. *Journal of Counseling Psychology, 48,* 274–285.

representation of lifelong goals, planning, or activity. The participants demonstrated a belief that career included a commitment, generally beyond what was necessary for a given job or type of work. In some instances, this commitment seemed to be part of the individual's self-identity. One woman responded, "It is your life" (Participant 1). Another participant discussed career as something she was born to do. "What I'm doing now, I have to do...[the Grandfather, or God] decided I will do this. I was born to do this. I will not do anything else" (Participant 13).

Note that the researchers name the number of participants with a particular point of view (i.e., 16 of the 18) in the example, which is superior to simply making a vague reference to "many," "a majority," or "some," which you will sometimes find in the results section of qualitative research reports.

Notice that Evaluation Question 3 does not merely ask whether examples are given; it asks whether they adequately support the statements of results. Thus, you will need to make judgments regarding whether there are sufficient numbers of examples and whether the examples are relevant to and supportive of the generalizations made by qualitative researchers. Making such judgments can be highly subjective but are a crucial aspect of evaluating qualitative research.

___ **4. When there are a number of statistics, have they been presented in table form?**

Very satisfactory 5 4 3 2 1 Very unsatisfactory *or* N/A I/I

Comment: Even when there are as few as six statistics, a table can be helpful. For example, if three groups are being compared, and there is a mean (the most common average) and standard deviation for each, a paragraph in which all these statistics are embedded could be hard to follow. On the other hand, a table in which all the means are in the same row or column enables a reader to quickly scan and compare them.

___ **5. If there are tables, are their important aspects discussed in the narrative of the results section?**

Very satisfactory 5 4 3 2 1 Very unsatisfactory *or* N/A I/I

Comment: Researchers should point out the important highlights of their statistical tables, as illustrated in Example 10.5.1. When there are large tables, pointing out the highlights can be especially helpful for consumers of the research.

Example 10.5.1[5]

A table with highlights discussed:

Total responses for time spent in recreational reading each week while classes are in session are shown in Table 1. While classes are in session, 63% of the respondents report reading 2 hours or less each week. At the other end of the continuum, only 13% of students surveyed report 6 or more hours per week when classes are in session.

Table 1   *Time spent reading recreationally: Classes in session*

Hours per week	Number of students	Percentage of students
Less than 1 hour	40	29
1–2 hours	47	34
3–5 hours	33	24
6–10 hours	12	8
More than 10 hours	7	5

___ **6. Have the researchers presented descriptive statistics before presenting the results of inferential tests?**

Very satisfactory 5 4 3 2 1 Very unsatisfactory *or* N/A I/I

Comment: Descriptive statistics includes frequencies, percentages, averages (usually the mean or median), and measures of variability (usually the standard deviation or interquartile range). In addition, correlation coefficients (usually the Pearson r) describe the direction and strength of relationships.

Inferential statistics determines the probability that any differences among descriptive statistics are due to chance (random sampling error). Obviously, it makes no sense to discuss the results of a test on descriptive statistics unless the descriptive statistics have first been presented. Failure on this evaluation question is very rare.

___ **7. If any differences are statistically significant and small, have the researchers noted that they are small?**

Very satisfactory 5 4 3 2 1 Very unsatisfactory *or* N/A I/I

Comment: Statistically significant differences are sometimes very small. (See Appendix C for an explanation of this point.) When this is the case, it is a good idea for a researcher to point this out. Obviously, a very small but statistically significant difference will be interpreted differently from a large and

---

[5] Gallik, J. D. (1999). Do they read for pleasure? Recreational reading habits of college students. *Journal of Adolescent & Adult Literacy, 42*, 480–488.

statistically significant difference. Example 10.7.1 illustrates how this might be pointed out.[6]

Example 10.7.1
Description of a small but statistically significant difference:

Although the difference between the means of the experimental group (*M* = 24.55) and control group (*M* = 23.65) was statistically significant (*t* = 2.075, *p* < .05), the small size of the difference, in absolute terms, suggests that the effects of the experimental treatment were weak.

This evaluation question is posed because researchers sometimes incorrectly believe that simply because a difference is statistically significant, it must be large enough to be important. They fail to understand that a significant difference is merely one that is unlikely to have been produced by chance. Note that there are no mathematical formulas (or tests) to determine the practical importance of a difference.

___ 8. Have appropriate statistics been selected?

Very satisfactory 5 4 3 2 1 Very unsatisfactory *or* N/A I/I

Comment: This is often a difficult question to answer because readers of reports typically do not have access to the original data, so they are unable to check for characteristics such as skewedness (if a distribution is highly skewed, the median should be preferred over the mean) or linearity (if the relationship between two variables is not linear, the Pearson *r* is inappropriate). This problem is compounded by the fact that very few researchers discuss whether they checked for such characteristics of their data before selecting statistics. Nevertheless, this evaluation question is posed because you may occasionally be able to spot the inappropriate selection of statistics.

___ 9. Overall, is the presentation of the results adequate?

Very satisfactory 5 4 3 2 1 Very unsatisfactory *or* N/A I/I

Comment: Rate this evaluation question after considering your answers to the earlier ones in this chapter and any additional considerations and concerns you may have.

---

[6] An increasingly popular statistic, *effect size*, is designed to draw readers' attention to the size of any significant difference. In general terms, it indicates by how many standard deviations two groups differ from each other. Unfortunately, its use is not very widespread to date.

Exercise for Chapter 10

Part A

Directions: Answer the following questions.

1. According to this chapter, should the results section of a quantitative report simply present statistics that "speak for themselves"? Explain.

2. Under what circumstance is a paragraph that describes the organization of the results section "highly desirable"?

3. According to this chapter, is it ever desirable to restate hypotheses that were originally stated in the introduction of a research report? Explain.

4. The results of qualitative studies should be supported with what type of material?

5. If statistical results are presented in a table, should all the entries in the table usually be discussed? Explain.

6. Should descriptive statistics *or* inferential tests be reported first in results sections?

7. Is it possible for a *small difference* to be a *statistically significant* difference?

Part B

Directions: Locate several research reports of interest to you in academic journals. Read them and evaluate the descriptions of the results in light of the evaluation questions in this chapter as well as any other considerations and concerns you may have. Select the one to which you gave the highest overall rating and bring it to class for discussion. Be prepared to discuss both its strengths and weaknesses.

Notes:

Chapter 11

Evaluating Discussion Sections

The last section of a report typically has the heading "Discussion." However, expect to see variations such as "Discussion and Conclusions" or "Conclusions and Implications."

___ **1. In long articles, do the researchers briefly summarize the purpose and results at the beginning of the discussion?**

Very satisfactory 5 4 3 2 1 Very unsatisfactory *or* N/A I/I

Comment: A summary at this point in a long article helps keep readers focused on the big picture. Example 11.1.1 shows the first paragraph of a lengthy discussion of a long research article. It points out the main purpose and general findings, which sets the stage for a more detailed discussion.

> **Example 11.1.1**[1]
> *Brief summary of study purpose and findings in the first paragraph of a discussion section*:
>
> This study explored the experiences of foster/adoptive parents who raise children diagnosed with FAS [Fetal Alcohol Syndrome]. Based on the findings, the potential role of family counselors in assisting these families was examined. When reflecting on the results of this study, it appears that family counselors can assist parents who face child management, relationship, and larger systems issues.

___ **2. Do the researchers acknowledge their methodological limitations?**

Very satisfactory 5 4 3 2 1 Very unsatisfactory *or* N/A I/I

Comment: Although the methodological limitations (i.e., weaknesses) may be discussed at any point in a research report, they are frequently included in the discussion section because any conclusions should be drawn in light of the limitations. These are sometimes discussed under the subheading "Limitations."

---

[1] Morrissette, P. J. (2001). Fetal alcohol syndrome: Parental experiences and the role of family counselors. *The Qualitative Report*, 6. Retrieved from http://www.nova.edu/ssss/QR/QR6-2/morrissette.html on January 13, 2003.

The two most common types of limitations are weaknesses in measurement (i.e., observation or instrumentation) and weaknesses in sampling. (See Guidelines 3 and 4 in Chapter 1.) Example 11.2.1 shows a portion of a discussion.

Example 11.2.1[2]

Acknowledgment of limitations in a discussion section:

Limitations of this study included the demographic restrictedness of the sample, the nonrepresentation of people residing in rural areas, the small proportion of respondents from racial or ethnic minority groups, and the complete reliance on self-report data. Much of the research on MS [multiple sclerosis] is criticized for these same shortcomings, and more information is needed on the impact of racial/ethnic, low income, and/or rural settings on employment outcomes.... Another potentially limiting feature was the coding of the employment status variable in a dichotomous (unemployed vs. employed) fashion. A more sensitive outcome variable for future research would be that of *employment involvement*, which may be operationalized in terms of the number of hours worked per week, days worked per month, or other indicators of job tenure.

___ 3. Are the results discussed in terms of the literature cited in the introduction?

Very satisfactory 5 4 3 2 1 Very unsatisfactory *or* N/A I/I

Comment: The literature cited in the introduction sets the stage for the report. It makes sense to finish the report by describing how the current study fits into the larger body of literature. Researchers might address issues such as: Are the results consistent with those in the literature? With only some of them? With none of them? Does this study fill a gap in the literature? These are important issues to consider when drawing conclusions from a particular study. For instance, if the results of a study being evaluated are inconsistent with the results of a large number of other studies in the literature, the researcher should discuss this discrepancy and consider speculating on why his or her study is inconsistent with earlier ones. Examples 11.3.1 and 11.3.2 illustrate how some researchers refer to literature that is cited in the introduction to their research reports.

---

[2] Roessler, R. T., Fitzgerald, S. M., Rumrill, P. D., & Koch, L. C. (2001). Determinants of employment status among people with multiple sclerosis. *Rehabilitation Counseling Bulletin*, *45*, 31–39.

Example 11.3.1[3]
Discussion in terms of literature mentioned in the introduction:

As for the research community, this study offered support to Aldrich and Zimmer (1986) and Tjosvold and Weicker (1993) who noted that developmental relationships could be of significant importance to women business owners for support in expanded knowledge, additional support, and alternative ideas. It also offered support to Kramer (1992) and Buttner and Rosen (1988) that female business owners do have a lack of business support networks. However, based on the focus group participants, male business owners also suffer from a lack of support networks.

Example 11.3.2[4]
Discussion in terms of literature mentioned in the introduction:

Why might our results differ so markedly from those of Lee and Bryk (1986) and others? One possibility is that something important about Catholic schools has changed since 1980.... Throughout the 1980s and early 1990s, a significant number of Catholic secondary schools...closed their doors while many other single-sex Catholic schools merged....

___ **4. Have the researchers avoided citing new references in the discussion?**

Very satisfactory 5 4 3 2 1 Very unsatisfactory *or* N/A I/I

Comment: The relevant literature should be first cited in the introduction. This is akin to laying all the cards on the table. The literature referred to in the discussion section should be limited to that originally cited in the introduction.

___ **5. Are specific implications discussed?**

Very satisfactory 5 4 3 2 1 Very unsatisfactory *or* N/A I/I

Comment: Research often has implications for practicing professionals. When this is the case, a statement of implications should describe, whenever possible, specifically what a person, group, or institution should do if the results of the study are correct. Depending on the particulars of a given study, researchers

---

[3] Gaskill, L. (2001). A qualitative investigation into developmental relationships for small business apparel retailers: Networks, mentors, and role models. *The Qualitative Report, 6*. Retrieved from http://www.nova.edu/ssss/QR/QR6-3/gaskill.html on January 13, 2003.
[4] LePore, P. C., & Warren, J. R. (1997). A comparison of single-sex and coeducational Catholic secondary schooling: Evidence from the National Educational Longitudinal Study of 1988. *American Educational Research Journal, 34*, 485–511.

may only be able to point consumers of research in a general direction as to how they might apply the results of research. In either case, it is inappropriate for researchers to assume that consumers of research will derive the implications without guidance because the implications are so obvious that they do not need discussion. Consumers of research will want to know what the researchers think the implications are and then evaluate whether they are appropriate. Example 11.5.1 is a sample statement of implications.

Example 11.5.1[5]
A statement of specific implications:

An important implication for practitioners working with Latino men is that these men reflect a variety of different masculinities. The challenge for the practitioner is to use whatever broad, general information about the Latino culture is available and apply it to the circumstances of the Latino client in developing an individualized assessment and treatment modality consistent with the client's cultural gender role perspectives. Generalizations about Latinos and their diverse masculinities are not valid and may therefore present an obstacle to engaging Latino men in a therapeutic working relationship.

Reaching out to include or expand mental health services to Latinos, particularly men, requires that consideration be given to the use of nontraditional treatment approaches targeted at deconstructing or redefining those meanings embedded in the "cult of masculinity." Formats for modifying or expanding gender role perspectives relevant to Latinos may focus on providing same-gender workshops, small groups or seminars, or psychoeducational classes promoting….

___ 6. Are the results discussed in terms of any relevant theories?

Very satisfactory 5 4 3 2 1 Very unsatisfactory *or* N/A I/I

Comment: As you know from earlier chapters, research that tests and/or develops theories is often important because theories provide the basis for numerous predictions and implications. If a study was introduced as theory driven (or even clearly based on certain theoretical considerations), it is appropriate to describe how the current results affect our interpretation of the theory in the discussion section at the end of the article. Example 11.6.1 shows a portion of such a discussion.

---

[5] Torres, J. B., Solberg, V. S. H., & Carlstrom, A. H. (2002). The myth of sameness among Latino men and their machismo. *American Journal of Orthopsychiatry, 72*, 163–181.

Example 11.6.1[6]

Discussion of the implications of the results of a study for theory:

Normative theory may have fallen out of vogue in recent decades, but these findings demonstrate the value of this traditional theoretical perspective. Social norms are powerful predictors of attitudes and behaviors, and prejudice and discrimination are no exception. One advantage of the normative approach is it allows for a pragmatic optimism. Rather than facing the daunting task of changing the ingrained attitudes of millions of individuals, a norms approach suggests that changing the normative climate can be an efficient and effective approach to attitude change (see Bem, 1970). The more desirable the group, the more people will wish to follow its lead. And when people identify with attractive groups that condemn a prejudice, they are likely to win the struggle for internalization.

___ 7. Are suggestions for future research specific?

Very satisfactory   5   4   3   2   1   Very unsatisfactory   *or*   N/A   I/I

Comment: It is uninformative for researchers to conclude with a simple phrase such as "more research is needed." To be helpful, researchers should point to specific areas and research procedures that might be fruitful in future research. This is illustrated in Example 11.7.1.

Example 11.7.1[7]

Specific suggestions for future research:

In sum, much more research is necessary to better understand and treat pathological gambling. First, greater knowledge of the onset and course of pathological gambling is needed. In the field of substance use disorders, early onset of use is associated with propensity to develop dependence (Hawkins et al., 1997). Because gambling initiates during or even prior to adolescence (Proimos et al., 1998), studies investigating early prevention efforts directed at high-risk populations may be useful. Numerous studies of substance abusers demonstrate an association between other psychiatric disorders and drug abuse. Similarly, for gamblers, more research is needed to assess whether affective and substance use disorders develop prior or subsequent to pathological gambling. Perhaps antidepressant treatment may be useful in the subset of gamblers whose depression preceded, rather

---

[6] Crandall, C. S., Eshleman, A., & O'Brien, L. (2002). Social norms and the expression and suppression of prejudice: The struggle for internalization. *Journal of Personality and Social Psychology, 82*, 359–378.

[7] Petry, N. M. (2002). How treatments for pathological gambling can be informed by treatments for substance use disorders. *Experimental and Clinical Psychopharmacology, 10*, 184–192.

than developed subsequent to, the gambling. Given the high rates of pathological gambling in treatment-seeking substance abusers, future studies should be directed at investigating treatments for dual diagnosis patients.

Second, better understanding of the physiology of pathological gambling also is needed. In particular, more studies characterizing withdrawal and tolerance may help inform whether medications may be useful during early stages of gambling cessation. If gambling results in physiological responses....

___ **8. Have the researchers distinguished between speculation and data-based conclusions?**

Very satisfactory   5   4   3   2   1   Very unsatisfactory   *or*   N/A   I/I

Comment: It is perfectly acceptable for researchers to speculate in the discussion section (e.g., what the results might have been if the methodology had been different). However, it is important that researchers clearly distinguish between their speculation and the conclusions that can be justified by the data they have gathered.

___ **9. Overall, is the discussion effective and appropriate?**

Very satisfactory   5   4   3   2   1   Very unsatisfactory   *or*   N/A   I/I

Comment: Rate this evaluation question after considering your answers to the earlier ones in this chapter and any additional considerations and concerns you may have.

Exercise for Chapter 11

Part A

Directions: Answer the following questions.

1. The methodological weaknesses of a study are sometimes discussed under what subheading?

2. What are the two most common types of limitations?

3. Example 11.2.1 is an excerpt from a study on the determinants of employment

status of individuals with MS. In the example, the researchers mention the "complete reliance on self-report data." Speculate on why they think this is a limitation.

4. Is it ever appropriate to mention literature that was cited earlier in a research article *again* in the discussion section at the end of a research article? Explain.

5. According to this chapter, when the implications of a study are obvious, should they be discussed anyway?

6. Suppose this was the entire suggestion for future research stated at the end of a research article: "Due to the less than definitive nature of the current research, future research is needed on the effects of negative political campaign advertisements." In your opinion, is this sufficiently specific? Explain.

7. Is it acceptable for researchers to speculate in the discussion section of their research reports? Explain.

Part B

Directions: Locate several research reports of interest to you in academic journals. Read them and evaluate the discussion sections in light of the evaluation questions in this chapter as well as any other considerations and concerns you may have. Select the one to which you gave the highest overall rating and bring it to class for discussion. Be prepared to discuss both its strengths and weaknesses.

Notes:

Chapter 12

Putting It All Together

If you have been faithfully applying the evaluation questions in Chapters 2 through 11, you have a series of "yes/no" answers and ratings from 1 to 5. Now it is time to put it all together and arrive at an overall evaluation. This should not be done in some mechanical manner such as summing the number of times you answered "yes." Instead, you should make an overall judgment by considering the research report as a "whole." The following evaluation questions are designed to help you do this.

___ **1. Have the researchers selected an important problem?**

Very satisfactory 5 4 3 2 1 Very unsatisfactory *or* N/A I/I

Comment: In Chapter 4, you were asked to consider whether the researchers established the importance of their problem. The evaluation question we are considering here is somewhat different from the one in Chapter 4 because this one asks whether, *in your judgment*, the problem is important—even if the researcher has failed to make a strong case for it. In other words, a researcher may have written an introduction that does not clearly establish the importance of the problem even though, in your judgment, it is an important one. In such a case, you would give the research report a high rating on this evaluation question but a low rating on Evaluation Question 2 in Chapter 4.

Note that a methodologically strong study on a trivial problem is a flaw that cannot be compensated for even with the best research writing and research methodology. On the other hand, a methodologically weak and poorly written study may, nevertheless, be judged to make a contribution—especially if there are no stronger studies available on the same topic or if there are no other studies on a topic that is of great current interest.

___ **2. Were the researchers reflective?**

Very satisfactory 5 4 3 2 1 Very unsatisfactory *or* N/A I/I

Comment: Researchers should reflect on their methodological decisions and share these reflections with their readers. This shows that careful thinking underlies their work. For example, do they reflect on why they worked with one kind of sample rather than another? Do they discuss their reasons for selecting one instrument over another for use in their research? Do they discuss their rationale for other design and procedural decisions they made in designing and conducting their research?

Researchers also should reflect on their interpretations of the data. Are there other ways to interpret it? Are the various possible interpretations described and evaluated? Do they make it clear why they favor one interpretation over another?

Such reflections can appear throughout research reports and often are repeated in the discussion section at the end.

___ 3. Is the report cohesive?

Very satisfactory 5 4 3 2 1 Very unsatisfactory *or* N/A I/I

Comment: Do the researchers make clear the heart of the matter (usually the research hypotheses, purposes, or questions) and write a report that revolves around it and is cohesive (i.e., flows logically from one section to another)? Note that a scattered, incoherent report has little chance of making an important contribution.

___ 4. Does the report extend the boundaries of our knowledge on a topic, especially our understanding of relevant theories?

Very satisfactory 5 4 3 2 1 Very unsatisfactory *or* N/A I/I

Comment: By introducing new variables or improved methods, researchers often are able to expand our understanding of a problem. It is especially helpful when their findings give us insights into various theories or provide data that may be used for theory development. When researchers believe their data clearly extends the boundaries of what we know about a research problem, they should state that they believe this is the case. Example 12.4.1 is from the introduction to a research report. The researchers state that their research has the potential to extend the boundaries of what we know as a partial justification for undertaking their research. Example 12.4.2 is excerpted from the discussion section of a research report in which the researchers state that their findings replicate and extend what is known about an issue. Note in footnote 2 that the title of the article from which the example was drawn uses the term "extension."

Example 12.4.1[1]

Researchers state in the introduction that their study will extend knowledge of the topic [emphasis added]:

There is a strong rationale for the development of interventions to assist with memory problems in early-stage Alzheimer's disease (AD). Despite severe episodic memory impairment, some components of memory are relatively preserved (Brandt & Rich, 1995), and a continued capacity for learning means that, given appropriate cognitive support (Bäckman, 1992), memory performance can be facilitated. This effect is evident both in relation to procedural (Zanetti et al., 1997, 2001) and verbal (Camp, Bird, & Cherry, 2000) memory tasks. A recent review of empirically validated treatments for older people (Gatz et al., 1998) classified "memory therapy" as "probably efficacious," indicating that it has some promise and that further research is warranted to *extend the evidence base and clarify outstanding questions*.

Example 12.4.2[2]

Researchers state in the discussion section that their study extended knowledge of the topic [emphasis added]:

The present findings must be replicated in future studies using more naturalistic tasks in nonlaboratory settings or with other behavioral assessments. However, it should be noted that the present finding of lack of Asian–White differences on behavioral indexes during a social performance task *replicates and extends the past findings* of verbal assertion with Chinese Americans using simulated role plays (D. Sue et al., 1983, 1990).

In some cases, a researcher may fail to point out that his or her research extends what we know, but *you may judge* that the research does extend it and give the research a satisfactory rating on this evaluation question. In other words, this evaluation question only asks whether the research extends what we know—not whether the researcher mentions the fact that it extends it.

____ **5. Are any major methodological flaws unavoidable or forgivable?**

Very satisfactory 5 4 3 2 1 Very unsatisfactory *or* N/A I/I

---

[1] Clare, L., Wilson, B. A., Carter, G., Roth, I., & Hodges, J. R. (2002). Relearning face–name associations in early Alzheimer's Disease. *Neuropsychology, 16,* 538–547.

[2] Okazaki, S., Liu, J. F., Longworth, S. L., & Minn, J. Y. (2002). Asian American–White American differences in expressions of social anxiety: A replication and extension. *Cultural Diversity and Ethnic Minority Psychology, 8,* 234–247.

Comment: No study is perfect, but some are more seriously flawed than others. When serious flaws are encountered, consider whether they were unavoidable. For example, getting a random sample of street prostitutes for a study on AIDS transmission is probably impossible. However, if the researchers went to the trouble to contact them at different times of the day in various locations (not just the safer parts of a city) and obtained a high rate of participation from those who were contacted, the failure to obtain a random sample would be forgivable because the flaw was unavoidable. Contrast this with researchers who want to generalize from a sample of fourth graders to a larger population but simply settle for a classroom of students who are readily accessible because they attend the university's demonstration school on the university campus. The failure to use random sampling or at least get a more diverse sample is not unavoidable and should be counted as a serious flaw.

Likewise, flaws in measurement (such as the unavailability of a highly valid instrument) or experimental design (such as the inability to assign at random for institutional or ethical reasons) may be forgivable.

Unless we tolerate some flaws under some circumstances, the vast majority of research in the social and behavioral sciences would need to be summarily rejected. Instead, as a practical matter, we tolerate certain flaws but interpret the data from seriously flawed studies with considerable caution.

___ 6. Is the research likely to inspire additional research?

Very satisfactory   5   4   3   2   1   Very unsatisfactory   *or*   N/A   I/I

Comment: Strong arguments for the importance of taking a closer look at a previously understudied problem, unique or improved methods that overcome flaws in previous studies, and interesting results that have practical and theoretical implications are likely to inspire additional research.

Even if a study is seriously flawed, its publication can be justified if it inspires others to study the problem—especially if they study it in different ways, with different samples, and, most important, with fewer major flaws. Keep in mind that research on a problem is an ongoing *process*, with each study contributing to our knowledge base. A study that stimulates the process and moves it forward is worthy of our attention—even if it is seriously flawed or is only a pilot study.

___ 7. Is the research likely to help in decision making?

Very satisfactory   5   4   3   2   1   Very unsatisfactory   *or*   N/A   I/I

Comment: Even seriously flawed research sometimes can help decision makers. Suppose a researcher conducted an experiment on a new drug-resistance educational program with no control group (usually considered a serious flaw) and found that students' illicit drug usage actually went up from pretest to posttest. Such a finding might lead the programs' funding agency to proceed cautiously before refunding or expanding the program, especially if other studies with different types of flaws produced results consistent with this one.

When applying this evaluation question, ask yourself how comfortable you would be making an important decision based on a study you are evaluating. In the absence of any other studies on the same topic, would this study help you make a more informed decision than if the study did not exist?

___ 8. **All things considered, is the report worthy of publication in an academic journal?**

Very satisfactory 5 4 3 2 1 Very unsatisfactory *or* N/A I/I

Comment: Given that space is limited in academic journals, with some journals rejecting more than 90% of the research reports submitted, is the report you are evaluating worthy of publication?

___ 9. **Would you be proud to have your name on the research article as a co-author?**

Very satisfactory 5 4 3 2 1 Very unsatisfactory *or* N/A I/I

Comment: This is the most subjective evaluation question in this book, and it is fitting that it is last. Would you want to be associated with the research you are evaluating?

Concluding Comment

I hope that as a result of reading and working through this book, you have become a critical consumer of research while recognizing that conducting solid research in the social and behavioral sciences is often difficult (and conducting "perfect research" is impossible).

Note that the typical research methods textbook attempts to show *what should be done in the ideal*. Textbook authors do this because their usual purpose is to train students in how to conduct research. Unless a student knows what the ideal standards for research are, he or she is likely to fall unintentionally into many traps. However, when evaluating reports of research in academic journals, it is unreasonable to hold each article up to ideal "textbook standards." Researchers conduct research under less-than-ideal conditions, usually with limited resources. In addition, they typically are forced to make many compromises (especially in measurement and sampling) given the practical realities of their research settings. A fair and meaningful evaluation of a research article takes these matters into consideration.

Appendix A[1]

Quantitative and Qualitative Research: An Overview

Because *quantitative* researchers reduce information to statistics such as averages, percentages, and so on, their research reports are easy to spot. If a report has a results section devoted mainly to the presentation of statistical data, it is a safe bet that it is a report of quantitative research. This approach to research has dominated the social and behavioral sciences throughout the 1900s, so for most topics, you are likely to locate many more articles reporting quantitative research than qualitative research.

The literature on how to conduct quantitative research *emphasizes*:

1. Starting with one or more very specific, explicitly stated research hypotheses, purposes, or questions, ideally derived from theory and/or previous research. Research plans focus narrowly on the stated hypotheses, purposes, or questions (as opposed to being wide ranging).
2. Selecting a random sample (like drawing names out of a hat) from a particular population so that the sample is representative of the population from which it was drawn.[2]
3. Using a relatively large sample of participants, sometimes as many as 1,500 for a national survey. Some quantitative researchers use even larger samples, but many use much smaller ones because of limited resources. A study with a large sample is usually a quantitative one. However, a study with a small sample could be either quantitative or qualitative.
4. Making observations with instruments that can be scored objectively, such as multiple-choice achievement tests and attitude scales in response to which participants mark choices such as "strongly agree" to "strongly disagree."
5. Presenting results using statistics, and making inferences to the population from which the sample was drawn (i.e., inferring that what the researcher found by studying a sample is similar to what he or she would have found by studying the entire population from which the sample was drawn).

---

[1] This appendix is based in part on material drawn with permission from Galvan, J. L. (1999). *Writing Literature Reviews: A Guide for Students of the Social and Behavioral Sciences*. Los Angeles: Pyrczak Publishing.

[2] It is "representative" except for the effects of random errors, which can be assessed with inferential statistics. Chapter 7 points out that researchers do not always sample or need random samples.

In addition, quantitative research is characterized by "distance" between researchers and their participants. That is, quantitative researchers typically have limited contact with their participants. In fact, it is not uncommon for the researcher to have no direct contact. For example, a quantitative researcher might have teachers administer tests to students without ever seeing or talking with the students. Even if the researcher is physically present in the research setting, he or she usually sticks to a script for the study and avoids unplanned personal interactions.

Qualitative research also has a long tradition in the social and behavioral sciences, but has gained a large following in many applied fields only in recent decades. It also is easy to spot, first, because the titles of the articles will often contain the word "qualitative." In addition, qualitative researchers usually identify their research as qualitative in their introductions as well as in other parts of their reports.[3] You can also spot it because the results section will be presented in terms of a narrative describing themes and trends—very often illustrated with quotations from the participants.

The literature on how to conduct qualitative research *emphasizes*:

1. Starting with a general research question or problem, and *not* formulating hypotheses derived from previously published literature or theories. Although qualitative researchers avoid starting with hypotheses, they may emerge (i.e., a researcher may formulate hypotheses that explain his or her observations) while conducting the research. Such hypotheses are subject to change as additional data are collected during the study. Thus, there is a fluid interaction between the data and any hypotheses.

2. Selecting a purposive sample—not a random one. A purposive sample is one in which the researcher has some special research interest and is not necessarily representative of a larger population. In other words, the researcher intentionally draws what he or she believes to be an appropriate sample for the research problem. For example, for a study of career development of highly achieving women, one group of researchers recently selected women who were identified in the media and by professional organizations as being leaders.[4] Thus, they were purposively identified—*not* selected at random.

3. Using a relatively small sample—sometimes as small as one exemplary case, but more often small groups of people or units such as classrooms, churches, and so on.

4. Observing with relatively unstructured instruments such as semistructured interviews, unstructured direct observations, and so on.

---

[3] Note that quantitative researchers rarely explicitly state that their research is quantitative. Because the overwhelming majority of research reports in journals is quantitative, readers will assume that it is quantitative unless told otherwise.

[4] Richie, B. S. et al. (1997). Persistence, connection, and passion: A qualitative study of the career development of highly achieving African American–Black and White women. *Journal of Counseling Psychology, 44*, 133–148.

5. Observing intensively (e.g., spending extended periods of time with the participants to gain in-depth insights into the phenomena of interest).
6. Presenting results mainly or exclusively in words, with an emphasis on understanding the particular purposive sample studied and usually de-emphasizing generalizations to larger populations.

In addition, qualitative research is characterized by the researchers' awareness of their own orientations, biases, and experiences that might affect their collection and interpretation of data. It is not uncommon for qualitative researchers to include in their research reports a statement on these issues and what steps they took to get beyond their own subjective experiences to understand their research problems from the participants' points of view. Thus, there is a tendency for qualitative research to be personal and interactive. This is in contrast to quantitative research, in which researchers attempt to be objective and distant.

As you can see from the above, the fact that the two research traditions are quite distinct will need to be taken into account when evaluating research reports. Because quantitative research is still by far the dominant type in academic journals, this book emphasizes its evaluation, with comments throughout when evaluation criteria may need to be modified for the evaluation of qualitative research. Those of you who are just beginning to learn about qualitative research are urged to read Appendix B in this book, which discusses some important issues in its evaluation.

Notes:

Appendix B

Examining the Validity Structure of Qualitative Research

R. BURKE JOHNSON
University of South Alabama

ABSTRACT. Three types of validity in qualitative research are discussed. First, descriptive validity refers to the factual accuracy of the account as reported by the qualitative researcher. Second, interpretive validity is obtained to the degree that the participants' viewpoints, thoughts, intentions, and experiences are accurately understood and reported by the qualitative researcher. Third, theoretical validity is obtained to the degree that a theory or theoretical explanation developed from a research study fits the data and is, therefore, credible and defensible. The two types of validity that are typical of quantitative research, internal and external validity, are also discussed for qualitative research. Twelve strategies used to promote research validity in qualitative research are discussed.

From *Education*, *118*, 282–292. Copyright © 1997 by Project Innovation. Reprinted with permission of the publisher and author.

Discussions of the term "validity" have traditionally been attached to the quantitative research tradition. Not surprisingly, reactions by qualitative researchers have been mixed regarding whether or not this concept
5 should be applied to qualitative research. At the extreme, some qualitative researchers have suggested that the traditional quantitative criteria of reliability and validity are not relevant to qualitative research (e.g., Smith, 1984). Smith contends that the basic epistemo-
10 logical and ontological assumptions of quantitative and qualitative research are incompatible, and, therefore, the concepts of reliability and validity should be abandoned. Most qualitative researchers, however, probably hold a more moderate viewpoint. Most qualitative re-
15 searchers argue that some qualitative research studies are better than others, and they frequently use the term validity to refer to this difference. When qualitative researchers speak of research validity, they are usually referring to qualitative research that is plausible, credi-
20 ble, trustworthy, and, therefore, defensible. We believe it is important to think about the issue of validity in qualitative research and to examine some strategies that have been developed to maximize validity (Kirk &

Miller, 1986; LeCompte & Preissle, 1993; Lincoln &
25 Guba, 1985; Maxwell, 1996). A list of these strategies is provided in Table 1.

One potential threat to validity that researchers must be careful to watch out for is called *researcher bias*. This problem is summed up in a statement a col-
30 league of mine once made to me. She said, "The problem with qualitative research is that the researchers find what they want to find, and then they write up their results." It is true that the problem of researcher bias is frequently an issue because qualitative research
35 is open-ended and less structured than quantitative research. This is because qualitative research tends to be exploratory. (One would be remiss, however, to think that researcher bias is never a problem in quantitative research!) Researcher bias tends to result from selec-
40 tive observation and selective recording of information, and also from allowing one's personal views and perspectives to affect how data are interpreted and how the research is conducted.

The key strategy used to understand researcher bias
45 is called *reflexivity*, which means that the researcher actively engages in critical self-reflection about his or her potential biases and predispositions (Table 1). Through reflexivity, researchers become more self-aware, and they monitor and attempt to control their
50 biases. Many qualitative researchers include a distinct section in their research proposals titled Researcher Bias. In this section, they discuss their personal background, how it may affect their research, and what strategies they will use to address the potential prob-
55 lem. Another strategy that qualitative researchers use to reduce the effect of researcher bias is called *negative case sampling* (Table 1). This means that they attempt carefully and purposively to search for examples that disconfirm their expectations and explanations about
60 what they are studying. If you use this approach, you will find it more difficult to ignore important information, and you will come up with more credible and de-

Table 1
Strategies Used to Promote Qualitative Research Validity

Strategy	Description
Researcher as "Detective"	A metaphor characterizing the qualitative researcher as he or she searches for evidence about causes and effects. The researcher develops an understanding of the data through careful consideration of potential causes and effects and by systematically eliminating "rival" explanations or hypotheses until the final "case" is made "beyond a reasonable doubt." The "detective" can utilize any of the strategies listed here.
Extended fieldwork	When possible, qualitative researchers should collect data in the field over an extended period of time.
Low inference descriptors	The use of description phrased very close to the participants' accounts and researchers' field notes. Verbatims (i.e., direct quotations) are a commonly used type of low inference descriptors.
Triangulation	"Cross-checking" information and conclusions through the use of multiple procedures or sources. When the different procedures or sources are in agreement, you have "corroboration."
Data triangulation	The use of multiple data sources to help understand a phenomenon.
Methods triangulation	The use of multiple research methods to study a phenomenon.
Investigator triangulation	The use of multiple investigators (i.e., multiple researchers) in collecting and interpreting the data.
Theory triangulation	The use of multiple theories and perspectives to help interpret and explain the data.
Participant feedback	The feedback and discussion of the researcher's interpretations and conclusions with the actual participants and other members of the participant community for verification and insight.
Peer review	Discussion of the researcher's interpretations and conclusions with other people. This includes discussion with a "disinterested peer" (e.g., with another researcher not directly involved). This peer should be skeptical and play the "devil's advocate," challenging the researcher to provide solid evidence for any interpretations or conclusions. Discussion with peers who are familiar with the research can also help provide useful challenges and insights.
Negative case sampling	Locating and examining cases that disconfirm the researcher's expectations and tentative explanation.
Reflexivity	This involves self-awareness and "critical self-reflection" by the researcher on his or her potential biases and predispositions as these may affect the research process and conclusions.
Pattern matching	Predicting a series of results that form a "pattern" and then determining the degree to which the actual results fit the predicted pattern.

fensible results.

65   We will now examine some types of validity that are important in qualitative research. We will start with three types of validity that are especially relevant to qualitative research (Maxwell, 1992, 1996). These types are called descriptive validity, interpretive validity, and theoretical validity. They are important to
70   qualitative research because description of what is observed and interpretation of participants' thoughts are two primary qualitative research activities. For example, ethnography produces descriptions and accounts of the lives and experiences of groups of people with a
75   focus on cultural characteristics (Fetterman, 1998; LeCompte & Preissle, 1993). Ethnographers also attempt to understand groups of people from the insider's perspective (i.e., from the viewpoints of the people in the group; called the *emic* perspective). Developing a theo-
80   retical explanation of the behavior of group members is

also of interest to qualitative researchers, especially qualitative researchers using the grounded theory perspective (Glaser & Strauss, 1967; Strauss and Corbin, 1990). After discussing these three forms of validity,
85   the traditional types of validity used in quantitative research, internal and external validity, are discussed. Internal validity is relevant when qualitative researchers explore cause and effect relationships. External validity is relevant when qualitative researchers gener-
90   alize beyond their research studies.

Descriptive Validity

The first type of validity in qualitative research is called *descriptive validity*. Descriptive validity refers to the factual accuracy of the account as reported by the researchers. The key questions addressed in descriptive
95   validity are: Did what was reported as taking place in the group being studied actually happen? and Did the

researchers accurately report what they saw and heard? In other words, descriptive validity refers to accuracy in reporting descriptive information (e.g., description of events, objects, behaviors, people, settings, times, and places). This form of validity is important because description is a major objective in nearly all qualitative research.

One effective strategy used to obtain descriptive validity is called *investigator triangulation*. In the case of descriptive validity, investigator triangulation involves the use of multiple observers to record and describe the research participants' behavior and the context in which they were located. The use of multiple observers allows cross-checking of observations to make sure the investigators agree about what took place. When corroboration (i.e., agreement) of observations across multiple investigators is obtained, it is less likely that outside reviewers of the research will question whether something occurred. As a result, the research will be more credible and defensible.

Interpretive Validity

While descriptive validity refers to accuracy in reporting the facts, interpretive validity requires developing a window into the minds of the people being studied. *Interpretive validity* refers to accurately portraying the *meaning* attached by participants to what is being studied by the researcher. More specifically, it refers to the degree to which the research participants' viewpoints, thoughts, feelings, intentions, and experiences are accurately understood by the qualitative researcher and portrayed in the research report. An important part of qualitative research is understanding research participants' inner worlds (i.e., their phenomenological worlds), and interpretive validity refers to the degree of accuracy in presenting these inner worlds. Accurate interpretive validity requires that the researcher get inside the heads of the participants, look through the participants' eyes, and see and feel what they see and feel. In this way, the qualitative researcher can understand things from the participants' perspectives and provide a valid account of these perspectives.

Some strategies for achieving interpretive validity are provided in Table 1. *Participant feedback* is perhaps the most important strategy (Table 1). This strategy has also been called "member checking" (Lincoln & Guba, 1985). By sharing your interpretations of participants' viewpoints with the participants and other members of the group, you may clear up areas of miscommunication. Do the people being studied agree with what you have said about them? While this strategy is not perfect, because some participants may attempt to put on a good face, useful information is frequently obtained and inaccuracies are often identified.

When writing the research report, using many low inference descriptors is also helpful so that the reader can experience the participants' actual language, dialect, and personal meanings (Table 1). A verbatim is the lowest inference descriptor of all because the participants' exact words are provided in direct quotations. Here is an example of a verbatim from a high school dropout who was part of an ethnographic study of high school dropouts:

> I wouldn't do the work. I didn't like the teacher and I didn't like my mom and dad. So, even if I did my work, I wouldn't turn it in. I completed it. I just didn't want to turn it in. I was angry with my mom and dad because they were talking about moving out of state at the time (Okey & Cusick, 1995: p. 257).

This verbatim provides some description (i.e., what the participant did) but it also provides some information about the participant's interpretations and personal meanings (which is the topic of interpretive validity). The participant expresses his frustration and anger toward his parents and teacher, and shares with us what homework meant to him at the time and why he acted as he did. By reading verbatims like this one, readers of a report can experience for themselves the participants' perspectives. Again, getting into the minds of research participants is a common goal in qualitative research, and Maxwell calls our accuracy in portraying this inner content interpretive validity.

Theoretical Validity

The third type of validity in qualitative research is called *theoretical validity*. You have theoretical validity to the degree that a theoretical explanation developed from a research study fits the data and, therefore, is credible and defensible. Theory usually refers to discussions of *how* a phenomenon operates and *why* it operates as it does. Theory is usually more abstract and less concrete than description and interpretation. Theory development moves beyond just the facts and provides an explanation of the phenomenon. In the words of Joseph Maxwell (1992):

> ...one could label the student's throwing of the eraser as an act of resistance, and connect this act to the repressive behavior or values of the teacher, the social structure of the school, and class relationships in U.S. society. The identification of the throwing as resistance constitutes the application of a theoretical construct...the connection of this to other aspects of the participants, the school, or the community constitutes the postulation of theoretical relationships among these constructs (p. 291).

In the above example, the theoretical construct called "resistance" is used to explain the student's behavior. Maxwell points out that the construct of resistance may also be related to other theoretical constructs or variables. In fact, theories are often developed by relating theoretical constructs.

A strategy for promoting theoretical validity is *extended fieldwork* (Table 1). This means that you should spend a sufficient amount of time studying your research participants and their setting so that you can have confidence that the patterns of relationships you believe are operating are stable and so that you can understand why these relationships occur. As you spend more time in the field collecting data and generating and testing your inductive hypotheses, your theoretical explanation may become more detailed and intricate. You may also decide to use the strategy called *theory triangulation* (Table 1; Denzin, 1989). This means that you would examine how the phenomenon being studied would be explained by different theories. The various theories might provide you with insights and help you develop a more cogent explanation. In a related way, you might also use investigator triangulation and consider the ideas and explanations generated by additional researchers studying the research participants.

As you develop your theoretical explanation, you should make some predictions based on the theory and test the accuracy of those predictions. When doing this, you can use the *pattern matching* strategy (Table 1). In pattern matching, the strategy is to make several predictions at once; then, if all of the predictions occur as predicted (i.e., if the pattern is found), you have evidence supporting your explanation. As you develop your theoretical explanation, you should also use the negative case sampling strategy mentioned earlier (Table 1). That is, you must always search for cases or examples that do not fit your explanation so that you do not simply find the data that support your developing theory. As a general rule, your final explanation should accurately reflect the majority of the people in your research study. Another useful strategy for promoting theoretical validity is called *peer review* (Table 1). This means that you should try to spend some time discussing your explanation with your colleagues so that they can search for problems with it. Each problem must then be resolved. In some cases, you will find that you will need to go back to the field and collect additional data. Finally, when developing a theoretical explanation, you must also think about the issues of internal validity and external validity to which we now turn.

Internal Validity

Internal validity is the fourth type of validity in qualitative research of interest to us. Internal validity refers to the degree to which a researcher is justified in concluding that an observed relationship is causal (Cook and Campbell, 1979). Often, qualitative researchers are not interested in cause and effect relationships. Sometimes, however, qualitative researchers are interested in identifying potential causes and effects. In fact, qualitative research can be very helpful in describing how phenomena operate (i.e., studying process) and in developing and testing preliminary causal hypotheses and theories (Campbell, 1979; Johnson, 1994; LeCompte & Preissle, 1993; Strauss, 1995; 1994).

When qualitative researchers identify potential cause and effect relationships, they must think about many of the same issues that quantitative researchers must consider. They should also think about the strategies used for obtaining theoretical validity discussed earlier. The qualitative researcher takes on the role of the detective searching for the true cause(s) of a phenomenon, examining each possible clue, and attempting to rule out each rival explanation generated (see *researcher as "detective"* in Table 1). When trying to identify a causal relationship, the researcher makes mental comparisons. The comparison might be to a hypothetical control group. Although a control group is rarely used in qualitative research, the researcher can think about what would have happened if the causal factor had not occurred. The researcher can sometimes rely on his or her expert opinion, as well as published research studies when available, in deciding what would have happened. Furthermore, if the event is something that occurs again, the researcher can determine if the causal factor precedes the outcome. In other words, when the causal factor occurs again, does the effect follow?

When a researcher believes that an observed relationship is causal, he or she must also attempt to make sure that the observed change in the dependent variable is due to the independent variable and not to something else (e.g., a confounding extraneous variable). The successful researcher will always make a list of rival explanations or rival hypotheses, which are possible or plausible reasons for the relationship other than the originally suspected cause. Be creative and think of as many rival explanations as you can. One way to get started is to be a skeptic and think of reasons why the relationship should not be causal. Each rival explanation must be examined after the list has been developed. Sometimes you will be able to check a rival explanation with the data you have already collected through additional data analysis. At other times you will need to collect additional data. One strategy would be to observe the relationship you believe to be causal under conditions where the confounding variable is not present and compare this outcome with the original outcome. For example, if you concluded that a teacher effectively maintained classroom discipline on a given day but a critic maintained that it was the result of a parent visiting the classroom on that day, then you should try to observe the teacher again when the parent is not present. If the teacher is still successful, you have some evidence that the original finding was not because of the presence of the parent in the classroom.

All of the strategies shown in Table 1 are used to improve the internal validity of qualitative research. Now we will explain the only two strategies not yet discussed (i.e., methods triangulation and data triangulation). When using *methods triangulation*, the researcher uses more than one method of research in a single research study. The word methods should be used broadly here, and it refers to different methods of research (e.g., ethnography, survey, experimental, etc.) as well as to different types of data collection procedures (e.g., interviews, questionnaires, and observations). You can intermix any of these (e.g., ethnography and survey research methods, or interviews and observations, or experimental research and interviews). The logic is to combine different methods that have "nonoverlapping weaknesses and strengths" (Brewer & Hunter, 1989). The weaknesses (and strengths) of one method will tend to be different from those of a different method, which means that when you combine two or more methods, you will have better evidence! In other words, the "whole" is better than its "parts."

Here is an example of methods triangulation. Perhaps you are interested in why students in an elementary classroom stigmatize a certain student named Brian. A stigmatized student would be an individual that is not well liked, has a lower status, and is seen as different from the normal students. Perhaps Brian has a different haircut from the other students, is dressed differently, or doesn't act like the other students. In this case, you might decide to observe how students treat Brian in various situations. In addition to observing the students, you will probably decide to interview Brian and the other students to understand their beliefs and feelings about Brian. A strength of observational data is that you can actually see the students' behaviors. A weakness of interviews is that what the students say and what they actually do may be different. However, using interviews you can delve into the students' thinking and reasoning, whereas you cannot do this using observational data. Therefore, the whole will likely be better than the parts.

When using *data triangulation*, the researcher uses multiple data sources in a single research study. "Data sources" does not mean using different methods. Data triangulation refers to the use of multiple data sources using a single method. For example, the use of multiple interviews would provide multiple data sources while using a single method (i.e., the interview method). Likewise, the use of multiple observations would be another example of data triangulation; multiple data sources would be provided while using a single method (i.e., the observational method). Another important part of data triangulation involves collecting data at different times, at different places, and with different people.

Here is an example of data triangulation. Perhaps a researcher is interested in studying why certain students are apathetic. It would make sense to get the perspectives of several different kinds of people. The researcher might interview teachers, interview students identified by the teachers as being apathetic, and interview peers of apathetic students. Then the researcher could check to see if the information obtained from these different data sources was in agreement. Each data source may provide additional reasons as well as a different perspective on the question of student apathy, resulting in a more complete understanding of the phenomenon. The researcher should also interview apathetic students at different class periods during the day and in different types of classes (e.g., math and social studies). Through the rich information gathered (e.g., from different people, at different times, and at different places) the researcher can develop a better understanding of why students are apathetic than if only one data source is used.

External Validity

External validity is important when you want to generalize from a set of research findings to other people, settings, and times (Cook and Campbell, 1979). Typically, generalizability is not the major purpose of qualitative research. There are at least two reasons for this. First, the people and settings examined in qualitative research are rarely randomly selected, and, as you know, random selection is the best way to generalize from a sample to a population. As a result, qualitative research is virtually always weak in the form of population validity focused on "generalizing to populations" (i.e., generalizing from a sample to a population).

Second, some qualitative researchers are more interested in documenting particularistic findings than universalistic findings. In other words, in certain forms of qualitative research the goal is to show what is unique about a certain group of people, or a certain event, rather than generate findings that are broadly applicable. At a fundamental level, many qualitative researchers do not believe in the presence of general laws or universal laws. General laws are things that apply to many people, and universal laws are things that apply to everyone. As a result, qualitative research is frequently considered weak on the "generalizing across populations" form of population validity (i.e., generalizing to different kinds of people), and on ecological validity (i.e., generalizing across settings) and temporal validity (i.e., generalizing across times).

Other experts argue that rough generalizations can be made from qualitative research. Perhaps the most reasonable stance toward the issue of generalizing is that we can generalize to other people, settings, and times to the degree that they are similar to the people, settings, and times in the original study. Stake (1990) uses the term *naturalistic generalization*[1] to refer to this process of generalizing based on similarity. The bottom line is this: The more similar the people and circumstances in a particular research study are to the ones that you want to generalize to, the more defensible your generalization will be and the more readily you should make such a generalization.

To help readers of a research report know when they can generalize, qualitative researchers should provide the following kinds of information: the number

[1] Donald Campbell (1986) makes a similar point, and he uses the term *proximal similarity* to refer to the degree of similarity between the people and circumstances in the original research study and the people and circumstances to which you wish to apply the findings. Using Campbell's term, your goal is to check for proximal similarity.

and kinds of people in the study, how they were selected to be in the study, contextual information, the nature of the researcher's relationship with the participants, information about any informants who provided information, the methods of data collection used, and the data analysis techniques used. This information is usually reported in the Methodology section of the final research report. Using the information included in a well-written methodology section, readers will be able to make informed decisions about to whom the results may be generalized. They will also have the information they will need if they decide to replicate the research study with new participants.

Some experts show another way to generalize from qualitative research (e.g., Yin, 1994). Qualitative researchers can sometimes use *replication logic,* just like the replication logic that is commonly used by experimental researchers when they generalize beyond the people in their studies, even when they do not have random samples. According to replication logic, the more times a research finding is shown to be true with different sets of people, the more confidence we can place in the finding and in the conclusion that the finding generalizes beyond the people in the original research study (Cook and Campbell, 1979). In other words, if the finding is replicated with different kinds of people and in different places, then the evidence may suggest that the finding applies very broadly. Yin's key point is that there is no reason why replication logic cannot be applied to certain kinds of qualitative research.[2]

Here is an example. Over the years you may observe a certain pattern of relations between boys and girls in your third-grade classroom. Now assume that you decided to conduct a qualitative research study and you find that the pattern of relation occurred in your classroom and in two other third-grade classrooms you studied. Because your research is interesting, you decide to publish it. Then other researchers replicate your study with other people and they find that the same relationship holds in the third-grade classrooms they studied. According to replication logic, the more times a theory or a research finding is replicated with other people, the greater the support for the theory or research finding. Now assume further that other researchers find that the relationship holds in classrooms at several other grade levels (e.g., first grade, second grade, fourth grade, and fifth grade). If this happens, the evidence suggests that the finding generalizes to students in other grade levels, adding additional generality to the finding.

We want to make one more comment before concluding. If generalizing through replication and theoretical validity (discussed above) sound similar, that is because they are. Basically, generalizing (i.e., external validity) is frequently part of theoretical validity. In other words, when researchers develop theoretical explanations, they often want to generalize beyond their original research study. Likewise, internal validity is also important for theoretical validity if cause and effect statements are made.

References

Brewer, J., & Hunter, A. (1989). *Multimethod research: A synthesis of styles.* Newbury Park, CA: Sage.

Campbell, D.T. (1979). Degrees of freedom and the case study. In T.D. Cook & C.S. Reichardt (Eds.), *Qualitative and quantitative methods in evaluation research* (pp. 49–67). Beverly Hills, CA: Sage Publications.

Campbell, D.T. (1986). Relabeling internal and external validity for applied social scientists. In W. Trochim (Ed.), *Advances in quasi-experimental design and analysis: New Directions for Program Evaluation, 31,* San Francisco: Jossey-Bass.

Cook, T.D., & Campbell, D.T. (1979). *Quasi-experimentation: Design and analysis issues for field settings.* Chicago: Rand McNally.

Denzin, N.K. (1989). *The research act: Theoretical introduction to sociological methods.* Englewood Cliffs, NJ: Prentice Hall.

Fetterman, D.M. (1998). Ethnography. In *Handbook of Applied Social Research Methods* by L. Bickman & D.J. Rog (Eds.). Thousand Oaks, CA: Sage.

Glaser, B.G., & Strauss, A.L. (1967). *The discovery of grounded theory: Strategies for qualitative research.* New York: Aldine de Gruyter.

Kirk, J., & Miller, M.L. (1986). *Reliability and validity in qualitative research.* Newbury Park, CA: Sage.

Johnson, R.B. (1994). Qualitative research in education. *SRATE Journal, 4*(1), 3–7.

LeCompte, M.D., & Preissle, J. (1993). *Ethnography and qualitative design in educational research.* San Diego, CA: Academic Press.

Lincoln, Y.S., & Guba, E.G. (1985). *Naturalistic inquiry.* Beverly Hills, CA: Sage.

Maxwell, J.A. (1992). Understanding and validity in qualitative research. *Harvard Educational Review, 62*(3), 279–299.

Maxwell, J.A. (1996). *Qualitative research design.* Newbury Park, CA: Sage.

Okey, T.N., & Cusick, P.A. (1995). Dropping out: Another side of the story. *Educational Administration Quarterly, 31*(2), 244–267.

Smith, J.K. (1984). The problem of criteria for judging interpretive inquiry. *Educational Evaluation and Policy Analysis, 6,* 379–391.

Smith, J.K. (1986). Closing down the conversation: The end of the quantitative-qualitative debate among educational inquirers. *Educational Researcher, 15,* 12–32.

Stake, R.E. (1990). Situational context as influence on evaluation design and use. *Studies in Educational Evaluation, 16,* 231–246.

Strauss, A. (1995). Notes on the nature and development of general theories. *Qualitative Inquiry 1*(1), 7–18.

Strauss, A., & Corbin, J. (1990). *Basics of qualitative research: Grounded theory procedures and techniques.* Newbury Park, CA: Sage.

Yin, R.K. (1994). *Case study research: Design and methods.* Newbury Park: Sage.

---

[2] The late Donald Campbell, perhaps the most important quantitative research methodologist over the past 50 years, approved of Yin's (1994) book. See, for example, his introduction to that book.

Appendix C

The Limitations of Significance Testing

Much of the research you evaluate will contain significance tests. They are important tools for quantitative researchers but have two major limitations. Before discussing the limitations, let us first briefly review the purpose of significance testing and the types of information it provides.

The Function of Significance Testing

The function of significance testing is to help us evaluate the role of chance errors due to sampling. Statisticians refer to these chance errors as *sampling errors*. As you will see later in this appendix, it is very important to note that the term *sampling errors* is statistical jargon that refers only to *chance* errors. Where do these sampling errors come from? They result from random sampling. Random sampling (e.g., drawing names out of a hat) gives everyone in a population an equal chance of being selected. Random sampling also produces random errors (once again, known as *sampling errors*). Consider Examples C.1 and C.2 to get a better understanding of this problem. Note in Example C.1 that when whole populations are tested, there are no sampling errors and, hence, significance tests are not needed. It is also important to note in this example that *a real difference can be a small difference* (in this example, less than a full point on a 30-item test).

Example C.1
Example with no sampling errors because a whole population of tenth graders was tested:

A team of researchers tested all 500 tenth graders in a school district with a highly reliable and valid current events test consisting of 30 multiple-choice items. The team obtained a mean (the most popular average) of 15.9 for the girls and a mean of 15.1 for the boys. In this case, the 0.8-point difference in favor of the girls is "real" because *all* boys and girls were tested. The research team did not need to conduct a significance test to help them determine whether the 0.8-point difference was due to studying just a sample of girls, which might not be representative of all girls, and a sample of boys, which might not be representative of all boys. (Remember that the function of significance testing is to help us evaluate the role of chance errors due to sampling.)

Example C.2

Example of sampling errors when in truth there is no difference between groups:

Suppose a different team of researchers conducted the same study with the same test at about the same time as the research team in Example C.1. (They did not know the other team was conducting a population study.) This second team drew a random sample of 30 tenth-grade girls and 30 tenth-grade boys and obtained a mean of 16.2 for the girls and a mean of 14.9 for the boys. Why didn't they obtain the same values as the first research team? Obviously, it is because this research team sampled. Hence, the difference in results between the two studies is due to *sampling errors*.

In practice, typically only one study is conducted using random samples. If researchers are comparing the means for two groups, there will almost always be at least a small difference (and sometimes a large difference). In either case, it is conventional for quantitative researchers to conduct a significance test, which yields a probability that the difference between the means is due to sampling errors. If there is a low probability that sampling errors created the difference (such as less than 5 out of 100 or $p < .05$), then the researchers will conclude that the difference is due to something other than chance. Such a difference is called a *statistically significant difference*.

The Limitations of Significance Testing

There are three major limitations to significance testing. Without knowing them, those who conduct and evaluate the results of quantitative research are likely to be misled.

First, *a significant difference can be large or small*. While it is true that larger differences tend to be statistically significant, significance tests are built on a combination of factors that can cancel each other out.[1] Under certain common circumstances, small differences are statistically significant. Therefore, the first limitation of significance testing is that it does not tell us whether a difference (or relationship) is large or small. (Remember that small differences can be "real" [see Example C.1], and these can be detected by significance tests.) The obvious implication for those who are evaluating research reports is that they need to consider the magnitude of any significant differences that are reported. For

---

[1] If the difference between two means is being tested for statistical significance, three factors are combined mathematically to determine the probability: the size of the difference, the size of the sample, and the amount of variation within each group. One or two of these factors can offset the other(s). For this reason, sometimes small differences are statistically significant, and sometimes large differences are *not* statistically significant.

instance, for the difference between two means, ask "By *how many points* do the two groups differ?" and "Is this a large difference?"

The second limitation of significance testing is that a statistical significance test does not indicate whether the result is of practical significance. For instance, a school district might have to spend millions of dollars to purchase computer-assisted instructional software to get a statistically significant improvement (which might be indicated by a research report). If there are tight budgetary limits, the results of the research would be of no practical significance to the district. When considering practical significance, the most common criteria are: 1) cost in relation to benefit of a statistically significant improvement (e.g., how many points of improvement in mathematics achievement can we expect for each dollar spent?), 2) the political acceptability of an action based on a statistically significant research result (e.g., will local politicians and groups that influence them such as parents approve of the action?), and 3) the ethical and legal status of any action that might be suggested by statistically significant results.

The third limitation is that statistical significance tests are designed to assess only sampling error (errors due to random sampling). More often than not, research published in academic journals is based on samples that are clearly not drawn at random (e.g., using students in a professor's class as research participants or using volunteers). Strictly speaking, there are no significance tests appropriate for testing differences when nonrandom samples are used. Nevertheless, quantitative researchers routinely apply significance tests to such samples. As a consequence, consumers of research should consider the results of such tests as exceedingly tenuous (i.e., merely suggestive).

Concluding Comment

Significance testing has an important role in quantitative research when differences are being assessed in light of sampling error (i.e., chance error). If researchers are trying to show that there is a real difference (when using random samples), their first hurdle is to use mathematics and the laws of probability to show that the difference is statistically significant. If they pass this hurdle, they should then consider how large the difference is in absolute terms (e.g., 100 points on College Boards versus 10 points on College Boards). Then, they should evaluate the practical significance of the result. If they used nonrandom samples, any conclusions regarding significance (the first hurdle) should be considered highly tenuous.

Because many researchers are more highly trained in their content areas than in statistical methods, it is not surprising that some make the mistake of assuming that when they have statistically significant results, by definition they have "important" results and discuss their results accordingly. As a savvy consumer of research, you will know to consider the absolute size of any differences as well as the practical significance of the results when evaluating their research.

Notes:

Appendix D

Checklist of Evaluation Questions

Below are the evaluation questions presented in Chapters 2 through 12 of this book. You may find it helpful to duplicate this appendix for use when evaluating research reports. Limited permission to do so is given on page *ii* of this book. Keep in mind that your professor may require you to justify each of your responses.

Chapter 2   Evaluating Titles

____ 1. Is the title sufficiently specific?

____ 2. Does the title indicate the nature of the research without describing the results?

____ 3. Has the author avoided using a "yes–no" question as a title?

____ 4. If there is a main title and a subtitle, do both provide important information about the research?

____ 5. Are the primary variables referred to in the title?

____ 6. Does the title indicate what types of people participated?

____ 7. If the title implies causality, does the method of research justify it?

____ 8. Is the title free of jargon and acronyms that might be unknown to the audience for the research report?

____ 9. If the study is strongly tied to a theory, is the name of the theory mentioned in the title?

____ 10. Overall, is the title effective and appropriate?

Chapter 3 Evaluating Abstracts

____ 1. Is the purpose of the study referred to or at least clearly implied?

____ 2. Does the abstract highlight the research methodology?

____ 3. Has the researcher omitted the titles of measures (except when these are the focus of the research)?

____ 4. Are the highlights of the results described?

____ 5. If the study is strongly tied to a theory, is the theory mentioned in the abstract?

____ 6. Has the researcher avoided making vague references to implications and future research directions?

____ 7. Overall, is the abstract effective and appropriate?

Chapter 4   Evaluating Introductions and Literature Reviews

____ 1. Does the researcher begin by identifying a specific problem area?

____ 2. Does the researcher establish the importance of the problem area?

____ 3. Are any underlying theories adequately described?

____ 4. Does the introduction move from topic to topic instead of from citation to citation?

____ 5. Is the research a coherent essay with logical transitions from topic to topic?

____ 6. Has the researcher provided conceptual definitions of key terms?

____ 7. Has the researcher indicated the basis for "factual" statements?

____ 8. Do the specific research purposes, questions, or hypotheses logically flow from the introductory material?

____ 9. Overall, is the introduction effective and appropriate?

Chapter 5   A Closer Look at Evaluating Literature Reviews

____ 1. If there is extensive literature on a topic, has the researcher been selective?

____ 2. Is the literature review critical?

____ 3. Is current research cited?

____ 4. Has the researcher distinguished between opinions and research findings?

___ 5. Has the researcher distinguished between what is proposed by a theory and research findings related to the theory?

___ 6. Overall, is the literature review portion of the introduction appropriate?

Chapter 6   Evaluating Samples When Researchers Generalize

___ 1. Was random sampling used?

___ 2. If random sampling was used, was it stratified?

___ 3. If the randomness of a sample is impaired by the refusal to participate by some of those selected, is the rate of participation reasonably high?

___ 4. If the randomness of a sample is impaired by the refusal to participate by some of those selected, is there reason to believe that the participants and nonparticipants are similar on relevant variables?

___ 5. If a sample from which a researcher wants to generalize was not selected at random, is it at least drawn from the target group for the generalization?

___ 6. If a sample from which a researcher wants to generalize was not selected at random, is it at least reasonably diverse?

___ 7. If a sample from which a researcher wants to generalize was not selected at random, does the researcher explicitly discuss this limitation?

___ 8. Has the author described relevant demographics of the sample?

___ 9. Is the overall size of the sample adequate?

___ 10. Is number of participants in each group sufficiently large?

___ 11. Has informed consent been obtained?

___ 12. Overall, is the sample appropriate for generalizing?

Chapter 7   Evaluating Samples When Researchers Do *Not* Generalize

___ 1. Has the researcher described the sample/population in sufficient detail?

___ 2. For a pilot study or developmental test of a theory, has the researcher used a sample with relevant demographics?

____ 3. Even if the purpose is not to generalize to a population, has the researcher used a sample of adequate size?

____ 4. If a purposive sample has been used, has the researcher indicated the basis for selecting individuals to include?

____ 5. If a population has been studied, has it been clearly identified and described?

____ 6. Has informed consent been obtained?

____ 7. Overall, is the description of the sample adequate?

Chapter 8   Evaluating Instrumentation

____ 1. Have the actual items, questions, and/or directions (or at least a sample of them) been provided?

____ 2. Are any specialized response formats, settings, and/or restrictions described in detail?

____ 3. When appropriate, are multiple methods used to collect data/information on each variable?

____ 4. For published instruments, have sources where additional information can be obtained been cited?

____ 5. When delving into sensitive matters, is there reason to believe that accurate data were obtained?

____ 6. Have steps been taken to keep the instrumentation from obtruding on and changing any overt behaviors that were observed?

____ 7. If the collection and coding of observations is highly subjective, is there evidence that similar results would be obtained if another researcher used the same measurement techniques with the same group at the same time?

____ 8. If an instrument is designed to measure a single unitary trait, does it have adequate internal consistency?

____ 9. For stable traits, is there evidence of temporal stability?

____ 10. When appropriate, is there evidence of content validity?

____ 11. When appropriate, is there evidence of empirical validity?

____ 12. Is the instrumentation adequate in light of the research purpose?

____ 13. Overall, is the instrumentation adequate?

Chapter 9   Evaluating Experimental Procedures

____ 1. If two or more groups are compared, were individuals assigned at random to the groups?

____ 2. If two or more comparison groups were *not* formed at random, is there evidence that they were initially equal in important ways?

____ 3. If only a single participant or a single group is used, have the treatments been alternated?

____ 4. Are the treatments described in sufficient detail?

____ 5. If the treatments were administered by individuals other than the researcher, were they properly trained?

____ 6. If the treatments were administered by individuals other than the researcher, was there a check to see if they administered the treatments properly?

____ 7. If each treatment group had a different person administering a treatment, has the researcher tried to eliminate the "personal effect"?

____ 8. Except for differences in the treatments, were all other conditions the same in the experimental and control groups?

____ 9. If necessary, did the researchers disguise the purpose of the experiment from the participants?

____ 10. Is the setting for the experiment "natural"?

____ 11. Has the researcher distinguished between *random selection* and *random assignment*?

____ 12. Has the researcher used ethical and politically acceptable treatments?

____ 13. Overall, was the experiment properly conducted?

Chapter 10   Evaluating Results Sections

____ 1. Is the results section a cohesive essay?

____ 2. Does the researcher refer back to the research hypotheses, purposes, or questions originally stated in the introduction?

___ 3. Are the results of *qualitative* studies adequately supported with examples of quotations or descriptions of observations?

___ 4. When there are a number of statistics, have they been presented in table form?

___ 5. If there are tables, are their important aspects discussed in the narrative of the results section?

___ 6. Have the researchers presented descriptive statistics before presenting the results of inferential tests?

___ 7. If any differences are statistically significant and small, have the researchers noted that they are small?

___ 8. Have appropriate statistics been selected?

___ 9. Overall, is the presentation of the results adequate?

Chapter 11 Evaluating Discussion Sections

___ 1. In long articles, do the researchers briefly summarize the purpose and results at the beginning of the discussion?

___ 2. Do the researchers acknowledge their methodological limitations?

___ 3. Are the results discussed in terms of the literature cited in the introduction?

___ 4. Have the researchers avoided citing new references in the discussion?

___ 5. Are specific implications discussed?

___ 6. Are the results discussed in terms of any relevant theories?

___ 7. Are suggestions for future research specific?

___ 8. Have the researchers distinguished between speculation and data-based conclusions?

___ 9. Overall, is the discussion effective and appropriate?

Chapter 12 Putting It All Together

___ 1. Have the researchers selected an important problem?

___ 2. Were the researchers reflective?

____   3. Is the report cohesive?

____   4. Does the report extend the boundaries of our knowledge on a topic, especially our understanding of relevant theories?

____   5. Are any major methodological flaws unavoidable or forgivable?

____   6. Is the research likely to inspire additional research?

____   7. Is the research likely to help in decision making?

____   8. All things considered, is the report worthy of publication in an academic journal?

____   9. Would you be proud to have your name on the research article as a co-author?

Notes:

Notes:

Notes:

Notes:

Notes: